"In *Fearless Loving*, Rhonda Britten's 8 Simple Truths deliver her trademark Fearbuster Exercises in a step-by-step plan any lover can use to review, enhance, and create loving relationships. This book will be a great addition to couples who want to be the best lovers they can be. A must for anyone serious about love."
—Lou Paget,
bestselling author of *The Big O*

"Eschewing simple and trite self-help solutions, Ms. Britten gives the reader thoughtful and creative approaches to conquering fear and doubt in order to love unencumbered. *Fearless Loving* is a well-written and enormously helpful book. Rhonda Britten weaves her personal experiences with those of her clients into a guide that is useful, compelling, and, above all, wise." —Dr. Fred Luskin,
director of the Stanford University Forgiveness Project, author of *Forgive for Good*

Praise for Rhonda Britten's
Fearless Living

"What Rhonda reveals and teaches is what every survivor has learned. Whether you are a Marine, recovering addict, fighting a major illness, or dealing with a significant physical or emotional loss, you [still] have a choice. You can learn from the pain . . . or continue to suffer. For those who haven't been truly educated and prepared for life, I suggest reading *Fearless Living* . . . Learning from the wisdom of others is the wise and easy way."
—Bernie Siegel, M.D.,
author of *Prescriptions for Living*

"*Fearless Living* helps you overcome all withholds and has you break through to greatness."
—Mark Victor Hansen,
coauthor of the *Chicken Soup for the Soul* series

continued on next page . . .

"For anyone wanting a bigger, richer life, *Fearless Living* is a rare gem that combines a mother lode of simple, practical tools, techniques and ideas with a walking, talking, 'been there' role model . . . Rhonda artfully blends her outstanding Fearbuster Exercises with stories that will hold your heart while you learn to live fearlessly."   —Lou Paget,
> author of *How to be a Great Lover*
> and *How to Give Her Absolute Pleasure*

"Rhonda Britten walks her talk—she IS fearless! There is no one better to share this powerful message and demonstrate how to move beyond fear and create success in every area of your life."   —Cynthia Kersey,
> author of *Unstoppable*

"In *Fearless Living*, Rhonda Britten has exposed fear for the imposter that it is. *Fearless Living* has the potential to neutralize any fear-based habits standing between you and the fulfillment of your destiny. Fear will flee in the face of your self-dominion as you master the powerful principles she has perfected through her own practice."   —Dr. Michael Beckwith,
> founder and spiritual director,
> Agape International Spiritual Center

"My life has catapulted since working with Rhonda. Things I used to fear barely get my attention. *Fearless Living* freed me to succeed. I believe *Fearless Living* is the answer to a lifetime of prayers."   —Linda Silvertsen,
> author of *Lives Charmed: Intimate Conversations*
> *with Extraordinary People*

FEARLESS
Loving

Eight Simple Truths That Will
Change the Way You
Date, Mate, and Relate

RHONDA BRITTEN

A PERIGEE BOOK

Most Perigee Books are available at special quantity discounts for bulk purchases for
sales promotions, premiums, fund-raising, or educational use. Special books, or book
excerpts, can also be created to fit specific needs.

For details, write: Special Markets, The Berkley Publishing Group, 375 Hudson Street,
New York, New York 10014.

To protect privacy, pseudonyms have been used
and certain characteristics have been disguised
in the case histories recounted.

A Perigee Book
Published by The Berkley Publishing Group
A division of Penguin Group (USA) Inc.
375 Hudson Street
New York, New York 10014

Dutton hardcover edition: January 2003
Perigee trade-paperback edition: January 2004

ISBN: 0-399-52942-X

Visit our website at
www.penguin.com

Library of Congress Cataloging-in-Publication Data

Britten, Rhonda.
Fearless loving : Eight simple truths that will change the way you date, mate,
and relate / Rhonda Britten.
p. cm.
ISBN 0-525-940707-8 (alk. paper)
1. Man-woman relationships. 2. Dating (Social customs) I. Title.
HQ801 B8563 2003
306.7—dc21   2002075910

Printed in the United States of America

10 9 8 7 6 5 4 3 2 1

To my dear sisters, Cindy and Linda.

Without their love, I would not be me.

Contents

Preface

What percentage of the day are you being true to yourself? Can you say "yes" when you mean yes and "no" when you mean no? Can you say "I love you" or "I'm sorry" without angst? Can you forgive yourself or someone else? Can you reach out to others when they are hurting and take care of yourself if you are on the receiving end of heartbreak?

Tell me the amount of time you spend being true to yourself, and I'll tell you how much fear is affecting your ability to give and receive love. On average, most people are true to themselves thirty percent of the time, while seventy percent of the time they make decisions based in fear. That means that seventy percent of the time, we look at the world through fear-colored glasses and make our decisions accordingly. No wonder love can seem elusive. I know that was true for me when I based all my decisions in fear. Living in fear can be addictive—and very lonely.

In my first book, *Fearless Living*, I talked about my personal journey from fear to fearlessness, as well as the journeys of quite a few clients. I described how fear silently and seductively shapes our perception of reality, and explained how we can shift our focus from fear to freedom. These days I spend much of my time traveling around the United States and the world sharing the ideas that inspired *Fearless Living* and showing people how to do it for themselves. My message is universal, because fear works the same way for everyone. It "protects" us by holding us back. It keeps us safe by keeping us small. It tells us not to be ourselves when that is all we've got. It confuses us by fogging the issues. Fear makes us cling to the familiar and build evidence against the new, the daring, and the different. Over the years, I have spoken with hundreds of thousands of people about how fear impacts their careers, their home life, even their bottom line. Again and again, one theme stands out above all the others: The biggest casualty of fear is love.

No matter where I am speaking, love is the first thing on almost everyone's mind. Whether I am in a meeting with the leaders of a Fortune 500 company, a workshop with administrative assistants, or a private session with a couple on the fritz, the big issue is always the same. Yes, people want to live fearlessly. They want to honor their true nature, stand up for themselves, and be a positive force in the world. Sure, they want to be more successful and live passionately with purpose. But above all, they want someone to share it with.

Our number-one human need is the desire to connect. From college girls to grandpas, that is what motivates our actions, thoughts, and feelings. I can be giving a speech on Fearless Leadership to a hall full of executives, and the moment I mention love or dating every head perks up and every hand starts scribbling notes. It never changes and it never slows down—love is what we long for. Fearless Love.

So when it came time to write my second book, I knew exactly what to do. Whether or not people had read *Fearless Living*, I wanted to give them the tools they need to find the kind of love they crave. The push and pull between love and fear affects all our actions, and once we are aware of that, we can consciously make choices that enhance our relationships. We can turn away from fear and toward love, just as we turn away from the shadows and step into the sunlight, if that is what we choose to do. We just have to know how to recognize sunlight when we feel it, and be willing to move. In *Fearless Loving*, I will provide the directions. You will provide the willing heart.

The Eight Truths in *Fearless Loving* are a distillation of what I have learned about relationships through my practice of Fearless Living and from the thousands of clients—singles and couples—who have come to me for advice about love. Together, these Eight Truths provide an approach that is drastically different from what you might be accustomed to. At the core of *Fearless Loving* is a simple concept: To get love, be love. It is a thought as ancient as the world's great philosophies. But how do you "be love"? Is it a spiritual trick that takes years to master? Not really. It's just a way of moving through the world, a path that reveals itself as soon as you become aware of how fear is influencing your perceptions. In *Fearless Loving* I will teach you how to recognize fear, master it, and "be love" every day. And the best part is that whether or not you are in a relationship, it's a lot more fun to "be love" than to "be fear."

The pain you suffer in relationships is a direct result of staying faithful to your fears and to a past that no longer serves you. Your unwillingness to grow is the painful part. When you are not satisfied, when you are unfulfilled, when you are frustrated, lonely, or angry, you must be willing to see things differently and make new choices and take new actions. I realize that this shift is a very big deal, especially if you have never been aware of the way fear undermines you. Maybe you never even knew you had a choice between fear and freedom. Maybe you didn't know how to tell the difference between a reaction and a decision, between drama and passion, between lust and love, between "yes" and "maybe" and "I don't know." After reading this book, you will be able to recognize the choices.

Or perhaps you are one of those people who thinks it's all a matter of luck or fate, and you just don't have what it takes. You're always standing in the wrong line. Maybe you've tried everything and have come to the conclusion that it's not going to happen for you. After you read this book, I am confident you will think differently. *Fearless Loving* may take you to a place you never anticipated, yet I promise that if you are willing to change your mind, you will also change your ability to find love, give love, and get love.

Then again, you might be eager to see things differently but unsure how to go about it. After reading this book, you will know. It all begins with Truth 1, "Love Is Up to You," where I introduce the basic concept behind *Fearless Loving*: The love in your life depends on how you perceive yourself. Self-acceptance is the key to changing your life experiences. In this chapter, I'll help you gain insight into your perceptions of yourself and others as we uncover your Love Legacy. Through this tool you will reground yourself in love, clarify what love means to you, and reach a fresh understanding of how your perceptions have influenced your relationships. The Love Legacy provides a launchpad for the rest of the Fearless Loving program.

Truth 2, "Everyone Is Innocent," presents the mind-set I believe is fundamental to Fearless Loving. We have been taught to watch our backs, be street smart, and stay alert for people who would harm us. This approach undermines love before it has a chance. Instead, why not assume that the world is on your side? I'll prove to you that this is not only the most gratifying way to live life, it is also the path most likely to lead to love. I'll introduce the concept of intention vs. expectation, and show you the Four Steps to Innocent Communication—how to talk, use empowering language, listen supportively, and invite the intimacy and trust you desire.

Is love a feeling or is it more? Truth 3, "Feelings Lie," explains how our culture encourages us to lose control and get swept away by feelings, ignoring the other elements that make up Fearless Love: commitment, actions, and intellect. In this chapter you will learn how to honor your feelings yet act on your commitments— the secret to making relationships last. For people who are confused by their own feelings, I provide a technique for understanding and naming them. I'll also teach you how to create the Love Log, a powerful tool for learning about yourself and those you love.

When it comes to love, the most overwhelming feeling of all is sexual desire. In Truth 4, "Chemistry Is Between Your Ears," you will learn how to delight in sex without being blindsided by it. Most people know there is a big difference between sexual attraction and true love, but not everyone is aware of the role that fear plays in binding us to the wrong people when sparks are flying. Sex is a thrilling part of any relationship, but true chemistry goes deeper than instant lust. This chapter shows you how to tell the two apart, and reveals why slow-burning chemistry often lasts the longest.

Truth 5, "Dating Is Where You Practice Being Yourself," is a groundbreaking six-step program that will give you the confidence and energy you need to meet new people, or reacquaint yourself with your partner, without feeling nervous, jaded, or powerless. I'll give you time limits, strategies, and guidelines that will keep you focused not just on your date but on your own growth. Dating shouldn't be a trial. At its best, it is a way of relaxing, making new friends, and learning a little more about yourself and the kind of love that is right for you. A special Dating Love Log keeps you focused and helps you decide whether to dive in or hold back.

Once you are in a relationship there are bound to be challenges, and nearly all of them involve boundaries. Truth 6, " 'Yes' Means Nothing If You Can't Say 'No,' " is the Fearless Loving guide to setting limits. It covers emotionally abusive relationships, establishing your non-negotiables, what's reasonable and what's not, understanding when you are violating someone else's boundary, and recognizing boundaries you didn't know you had. I also provide a five-step strategy for setting and enforcing boundaries.

One of the main reasons people hesitate to fall in love is that they fear losing the relationship. Most of us have been hurt before and don't want to feel that pain again. Truth 7, "Loss Is a Fact of Love," tackles the reality of loss head-on. There is no love without loss, even in the most committed relationships. More to the point, we must be able to process losses we've had in the past in order to love again. I know from experience how hard this is, and I also know that it can be done. I will show you strategies I have used to recover from terrible loss, and will share with you stories of people who have used these techniques to work through divorce, death, betrayal, and the loss of the soul mate fantasy. You'll learn how to fortify yourself, regain trust in your own judgment, and accept the losses that will come, in some form, with every love you experience.

Truth 8, "Love Is a Risk You Must Take," lays it all on the table. Risk scares us, and loving someone is risky. We could lose, we could be hurt, we could be disappointed. But we could also be amazed, overjoyed, fulfilled, and at peace with life. In the end, the choice is ours. We can trust fear, or we can trust love. We can expand our view of ourselves, give up our narrow expectations of others, and open our hearts to a broader perception of love. Love thrives in the unknown, and the unknown can be frightening. But the Fearless Loving Truths act as a compass, making risk feel less like a threat and more like an adventure. This final chapter is full of stories and insights that will inspire you to stay on the fearless path—loving yourself, loving life, and being love.

The Fearbuster Exercises in *Fearless Loving* are going to surprise and enlighten you. The Eight Truths will radically alter your concept of love. If you've been looking for a way to break out of the cynical, same old, safe and stale approach to relationships, you have just found it. Bring your fearless heart, and let's get going!

Love Is Up to You

L ove is messy. It is rarely what we think it should be, and we are rarely what we would like to be when we are in love. On one hand we want love to be enough. Yet, on the other hand, we are rarely satisfied with the love we have. So fear and love battle it out.

We become silent when we desperately want to connect. We jump in too fast when we know we must slow down. We act cool when we feel hot. We wake up in the middle of the night to snuggle next to the one we love, yet we barely touch each other during the day. We shout in anger as we pray for patience. We put on an act, then worry we won't be loved for who we really are. We reach out. We shut down. We cry. We run. We doubt. Yet we can't live without it.

Love is messy. It won't be confined to our preconceived ideas. We want love to just happen, but love is not convenient. Its highs are higher and its lows are lower than we are ever prepared for. Love requires more of us than we think we can give. It pushes us past our breaking point, and yet we don't break. It is unpredictable, then sedate. It tears us up while making us better. It is never what we expect.

1

Love is messy because our desire for love is driven by our fears. We fear being rejected, so we become people-pleasers and call it love. We fear seeming inadequate, so we look for a partner who is perfect and call it having high standards. We fear looking stupid, so we keep to ourselves when our soul yearns to open up. We fear we are unlovable, so we hide our true self from those we love. We are afraid to be without love, but many times we are more afraid to be in love.

What percentage of your loving relationships are run by fear? When you are willing to see how fear has been running your love life, being and staying in love becomes a whole lot easier. Love is messy. Embrace it. Face it. And love will reveal itself in ways you could never imagine. Because ultimately, love will save you from your fears and show you the way home.

The Eight Truths in *Fearless Loving* were inspired by my own experiences with love as well as the thousands of hours I have spent coaching singles and couples who are trying to uncover love's mysteries. I have guided some of these people through painful breakups, to romance, and on to marriage. I have shown others how to love themselves enough to leave a bad relationship. I have proven to many couples that they can heal their love when they understand their fears and are willing to be vulnerable. At the heart of what I have learned is the simple fact that love begins with you. Loving yourself, no matter what, is the secret of how to give love, get love, and be love. And the only thing standing between you and love is fear.

Loving is a verb. It is what we "do." It is who we are at the core of our being. When we are fearless, loving is what we do best. Just as *Fearless Living* explained what fear is and how it blocks us, *Fearless Loving* will show you how, when you're willing to love yourself, you can love others and be loved. It all comes down to you. You are the common denominator in your life. You were there during each of your relationships. You were there when you were being romantic, angry, or unsure. You are the one who is choosing how much or how little love you feel. Once you face your fears and accept yourself, I know you will be able to step into the flow of love that exists everywhere. It won't matter that love is messy, because you will stay centered due to the love within you, not the love you receive.

When you are free of fear and able to love yourself, you will discover that you really can trust life. You will be able to act loving with no thought of getting anything in return. The act itself provides the gift. The kindness produces strength. The willingness to reveal your humanity enables you to connect with other people the way you have always longed to. When you can act loving despite your mood, your "evidence" about the world, and your situation in life, that is when you become completely aligned with your destiny. Nothing can stand in your way, and nothing can keep love from finding you.

My Crash Course In Fear

For most of my life, I could have been a poster girl for the opposite of all the traits I just described. Trust life? I was terrified. Far from revealing my humanity and vulnerability to others, I pushed friends away with my outrageous expectations of them. It helped protect me from anyone finding out the truth, as I perceived it: that I was a loser who would never be loved. Deep down, I believed I was not worth loving. If I was, how could my father have committed the crime that had shattered my world when I was a teenager?

3

My father and I had never gotten along. Even as a small child I had resented the way he tried to control my mother, my two sisters, and me. I can actually recall him counting toilet paper sheets to make sure my mom was staying within her budget. He was insecure and envious of her easy laugh and bright smile. His feelings for his family ran hot and cold, and that was especially true for me. I was definitely not his favorite. He often told me I was too loud, too smart for my own good, or just "too much."

When I was young, we had very little money and lived in a one-bedroom house. My sisters and I shared the bedroom and our parents slept in the living room. My father worked at a computer company, and to help make ends meet my mom ended up taking a job as a waitress. With her vivacious personality she made loads of tips, and soon she was earning more than my father. That's when he struck his first blow. At one point, convinced that she had to be doing more than just waitressing to earn all that money, he beat her so severely that she ended up in the hospital. It proved effective. After that, he hardly had to threaten her again. He just had to give her "the look" and she would get right in line.

When I was twelve, he began to turn his anger on me. I made some smart-aleck remark and suddenly he had his hands around my throat and was strangling me. I got loose only with the help of my younger sister Linda, Daddy's little favorite. She screamed at him, begging, "Please, Daddy, quit killing Rhonda." Finally he let go. I was left gasping for breath and wondering for the millionth time what was wrong with my father, or for that matter, my mother. Why didn't she make him leave? As a child, I didn't know about the fears that keep so many women in abusive marriages—fear of being unable to support your children; fear of making them the target of your husband's rage; fear of being shunned by the community and seen as a bad mother or worse.

Yet two years later my mom actually did it. She made my father move out of our house and started quietly arranging for a divorce. He did not take this lightly, but somehow she managed to shield us from the worst of his tirades. When he arrived at our doorstep on Father's Day, 1975, we had agreed to go out together as a family for Sunday brunch. I was waiting on the front porch when my mother slipped past us to open her car door. My father, who appeared calm and composed for a change, watched her. Then he followed her through the light rain, mumbling something about wanting to get a coat from his car. He unlocked his trunk, reached inside, and pulled out a rifle instead. As my mother turned toward him, he aimed it at her and shouted, "You made me do this!" She yelled, "Put down that gun!" He shot her in the stomach. Doubled over, she looked straight at me, crying out in shock and pain. He swung the gun toward me, and I thought I was next for sure. Instead, he swung it back toward my mother and shot her one more time. The second bullet went clear through her, landing in the car horn, which started blaring through my screams. I saw my mom fall back through the open car door. The next thing I knew my father was walking toward me. Sliding onto his knees just a few feet away, he put the rifle to his temple and fired.

It must have taken only a minute or two, but it felt like eternity. Through it all I stood frozen on the porch, screaming, "No, Dad! Please stop! No!" But I didn't move an inch. My sisters, who had been inside, had heard the shots and run across the street to get help. I rushed into my mother's room, knelt down next to her bed, and prayed feverishly for her to be alive. In a few minutes the police arrived. An officer found me curled against the bed, pulled me gently to my feet, and guided me to the living room.

It seemed like forever until the ambulance finally pulled up. The police had kept us away from our parents, and now the paramedics draped their bodies and loaded them inside. No one would let me see my mom. I sat on the couch with my sisters and realized that the life I had wished for myself would never happen. It was gone now. I would never be the girl I was meant to be. And I knew, somehow, that it was all my fault.

To take the edge off my grief, I called my boyfriend and begged him to come over. He and his father were there in minutes, but when they walked into the room it was clear they didn't know how to handle the situation. His father murmured, "It's not our place to be here now," and they left. My pain swelled into an awful foreboding. Here we go, I thought. No one will ever want to be with me again. I will be "too much," just as my father had always said. From that moment on, I feared I would always be alone.

That night my sisters and I stayed at my aunt's house. I slept on the top bunk of a double-decker bed, my cousin Donna sleeping underneath. When the lights went out I couldn't hold it in any longer. I cried hysterically, kicking the wall and screaming, "Why? Why? Why?" But there would be no crying in public. I knew from the very beginning that people would be afraid of such strong emotions. They wouldn't want to be with me, just as my boyfriend hadn't. I was marked as the girl who had watched her parents die.

The tragedy left me with a profound fear that I did not deserve to be alive, much less loved. It left me convinced I was a loser. Perhaps I had willed my father's death by wishing so many times that he were gone. And what about my mother? She was the only person I was sure had loved me and now she was dead because of my incompetence. I had not been quick enough to save her. It had been confirmed: I was not good enough. And I was afraid anyone who knew me would eventually find out.

As I grew up, this fear continued to rule every waking hour, distort every feeling, and sabotage every relationship. It drove me to be a perfectionist and expect things of myself no one could possibly achieve. It pushed me to drink too much, spend too much, and work too much. It urged me to put the people who might love me through endless tests so I could be sure they did love me. Of course, I made the tests impossible to pass. In my fear and hopelessness, I tried three times to take my own life.

Desperate to come to terms with my parents' deaths, I kept looking for some sort of cure. I tried therapy, grief groups, books, and courses. Nothing worked, but through these attempts I made a remarkable discovery. Fear itself was at the root of my troubles. Not the memories of the murder/suicide, not the years of feeling guilty and worthless, and not the overworking, drinking, and spending sprees I indulged in to numb my pain. Those were only symptoms of the unconscious fear that was running my life. Although I had tried to change these self-destructive behaviors through willpower, it had never worked because the core of my problem was the primal fear that I was a loser, *I was not good enough*. The only way out of my despair would be to identify that fear every time it erupted and change the way I responded to it.

Eventually I became aware that there were two Rhondas: one who experienced moments of ease, synchronicity, and peace, and one who reacted out of fear. One Rhonda knew who she was, but that Rhonda hardly ever saw the light of day. It seemed I could never stay in that state of mind. The second Rhonda was busy pretending to be someone she wasn't because of her distaste for who she thought she was—a loser. But even though I only rarely experienced my better self, that self was the true me. I realized that the way to get to this essential me was *through* the fear. Instead of denying it or running from it, I had to learn how to face it and transform it.

Wheel of Freedom, Wheel of Fear

Once I found a possible light at the end of the tunnel, I was eager to learn more about fear. I read everything I could get my hands on, and still do. The connection between fear and behavior is obvious and well documented, but what I find most exciting is the research about fear and consciousness. In his excellent book *Fear Itself,* Rush W. Dozier, Jr., talks about three fear systems: the primitive system, the rational system, and consciousness itself, which he believes is the most powerful system of all. According to Dozier, consciousness is "nature's fantastically advanced evolutionary response to the problem of fear . . . Most of the problems fear causes in our personal lives . . . arise from our failure to use the mental resources of the conscious mind to keep our primitive emotions in check. We now know techniques that enable consciousness and the rational fear system to control these fears effectively. Such scientifically proven techniques allow people literally to rewire their brains and alter their thought patterns."

Fear Itself confirms what I have discovered in my work with Fearless Living. At the heart of my program is the belief that each of us can achieve personal freedom and attain our goals by understanding what we are afraid of, identifying our essential nature, and consciously steering these two forces. The tools I created to help do this are called the Wheel of Fear and the Wheel of Freedom. They are the cornerstones of the Fearless Living program, and I describe them in detail in the Appendix.

Let me share a brief explanation of how these tools work. The Wheel of Fear is a result of your family heritage, belief system, and life experiences. It is a vicious cycle composed of a fear trigger (any event that triggers your fear of not being good enough), your response to that fear, the negative feelings that well up when the response fails to soothe the fear, and the self-destructive behavior you engage in to numb the pain of all of the above. By recognizing when your Wheel of Fear is being activated, you can consciously change your behavior.

The Wheel of Freedom is not the opposite of the Wheel of Fear, it is an alternate cerebral pathway. Using the Wheel of Freedom, you are able to access your *essential nature*—the you that feels authentic, powerful, and in tune with life. Your essential nature is often the one part of yourself that you deny, usually because you long to possess this quality above all others but believe you don't have it in you. In *Fearless Living*, I show you how to identify your essential nature—it could be creative, compassionate, accountable, courageous, or any number of other traits. Your essential nature is the first point on your Wheel of Freedom. Once you have identified it, you can engage in the second point: proactive behavior that reinforces your essential nature. This in turn leads to the third point on the wheel, a feeling of wholeness. The fourth point on the Wheel of Freedom, self-affirming behavior, is the result of consciously choosing freedom over fear. In this way, the Wheel of Freedom rewires your brain and alters your thought patterns.

In *Fearless Loving* I will teach you how to take the power of the Fearless Living program to the next level—personal relationships—so that your connections with lovers, spouses, friends, and family will be cleaner, more joyful, and more full of promise.

Your First, Best Love

You've heard it countless times before: "You have to love yourself before anyone can love you." But what does that mean? How many of us really love ourselves, and should we wait around until we do before we let someone else love us?

I'd estimate that maybe two percent of the people I have met love themselves. The other ninety-eight percent like themselves now and then, beat themselves up too much, and often wonder whether they deserve the love they have. In other words, they're human. Yet there is truth to the idea that you have to love yourself in order to *believe* someone worthwhile will love you. By loving yourself I don't mean indulging your every whim and thinking nonstop about you, you, you. It has nothing to do with narcissism. It's about self-acceptance.

Are you fond of yourself? Can you look in the mirror and feel warmth and affection for the person standing there? Can you acknowledge everything you have accomplished, and are you proud of it? Can you forgive yourself for all the mistakes you think you have made and the opportunities you think you have missed? Do you like yourself just as you are? Are you steadily moving forward at your own pace, confident that you are doing just fine?

If you can't answer yes, you will have a very hard time acknowledging, accepting, being proud of, and loving someone else. You will find it almost impossible to believe someone can love you. Because the love that comes into your life depends on you—how you perceive yourself, how you treat yourself, and how you treat other people. Love exists. Love is within you and around you. To see it, you need only be willing to change your view of yourself.

As I developed Fearless Living, I had to face some of the personal limitations I had always tried to deny. I'm a procrastinator and a perfectionist, and I have a tendency to set unrealistic deadlines. I overthink things. I overbook myself. I still occasionally wrestle with my longtime fear of not being good enough. But now, instead of berating myself for these traits, I accept them. I watch my thoughts, actions, and feelings without either approving or condemning them. When this behavior comes up I don't think, "This can't be me!" I think, "This is me under these circumstances." Then I ask myself, "What am I learning about myself in this situation? Are there boundaries I must put in place? Am I willing to see this situation, and myself, through the eyes of love?" The moment I see myself as I am rather than wishing I were different is the moment I become self-accepting.

In accepting myself, I am open to continually learning new things about me. I have learned that I can choose to change, ask for help, and love myself more. I have a hard time with overcommitment, so I learned to team up with other people and found that I work best that way—I get more done when I have someone to bounce ideas off. When I overthink things and blow a situation all out of proportion, I talk myself back to freedom by admitting out loud, "I just made that up." I try to respond to every event in my life, both internal and external, in a way that honors my essential nature, authenticity. By doing that I have been able to accept myself and, yes, even love myself.

Self-acceptance. Self-love. Self-approval. Fear teaches you that you don't deserve any of them. It tries to protect you from disappointment by telling you to put yourself down before anyone else has the chance to do it. It whispers that no one could love the real you. It warps your definition of love so that it doesn't include the most important person—you! Until now, you may have gone along with this fiction. No more.

Together, we will discover how loving yourself, loving other people, and receiving love are all bound together. Love is what you naturally express when you are comfortable and confident in your own skin. You don't have to earn or deserve love. You *are* love. Loving is never about how others treat you. It is always about how you are treating yourself, and how you share the overflow with others.

Your Love History

How do you activate love? By understanding that you have love within you already. You have a reservoir you can draw from. To give you a jump-start, I want you to go back in time to complete the Fearbuster Exercise below. If you don't think you remember, fill in the first name that pops into your head. It could be a teacher or a member of your extended family, your minister, or a friend's mom. Your subconscious remembers, so go with your first reaction.

Fearbuster Exercise: Who Loved You When You Were Growing Up?

Who . . .

_____ hugged you for no reason at all

_____ kissed you good night

_____ showed you how to fight fair

_____ dried your tears

_____ read your favorite bedtime story

_____ asked you how school was

_____ cheered you on

_____ took you to the park (or another special place)

_____ attended your events

_____ came to graduation

_____ encouraged you to get better grades

_____ told you they loved you

_____ held your hand when you were scared

_____ helped you make friends in the neighborhood

_____ introduced you to consequences

_____ laughed at your jokes

_____ missed you

_____ cooked your favorite meal or baked your favorite cookies

_____ brought you ginger ale when you were sick

_____ rubbed your head when it hurt

_____ celebrated birthdays

_____ cried when you left home

_____ told you, "you are beautiful, handsome, smart, amazing . . ."

_____ tucked you into bed

_____ washed your clothes

_____ gave you the opportunity to work as part of a family

_____ told you, "you can do it"

_____ answered your questions without making you feel dumb

_____ listened

_____ believed in you

Like most people, I wrote only a few names on my Love History list. A few is all you need. And even one name is enough. Sometimes we take these first loves for granted (*"Of course* my mother loves me—what does she know? I'm her child!"*) but obviously they are crucial to our sense of self-worth and lovability.

As important as our childhood relations are, the people who love us when we grow up are just as relevant to our love history. My friend Marta, whom you may have read about in *Fearless Living*, was the first person in my adult life to love me unconditionally (other than my sisters). As my surrogate mother, she was able to see past my self-betrayal and encourage me to discover who I truly was. Others may have tried to help, but I couldn't see or accept it. I had to be ready. Unconditional love is a powerful healing force and a rare gift. With her willingness to see me as fearless, Marta showed me another way love could look. Maybe there are people who have given you the same gift. Fill in their names below.

 Fearbuster Exercise: Who Loves You Now?

Who . . .

_____ misses you when you are away

_____ brings you chicken soup when you are ill

_____ drives you to the airport

_____ hugs you

_____ loves you unconditionally

_____ kisses you hello

Love Is Up to You

_____ calls you for no reason

_____ stands beside you

_____ supports your dream

_____ helps you find your way

_____ encourages you to keep going

_____ sends you love notes

_____ sees the best in you

_____ listens without judgment

_____ tells you the truth

_____ celebrates your successes

_____ reaches for you in the middle of the night

_____ applauds your courage

_____ enjoys your eyes and smile

_____ chooses to see your greatness when you cannot

_____ laughs with you

_____ dries your tears

_____ pushes you to be more

_____ does the little things

_____ accepts you for who you are

_____ cares for you

_____   wants you to love you more than them

_____   admires your power

_____   doesn't try to change you

_____   gives you the best surprises

_____   believes in you

Perhaps the names on your lists are not family members. That's how it is for me. Marta isn't a member of my family, although I feel as close to her as if she were. And then there was Mr. Berini, my high school counselor. After my parents died, he was one of the few people who reached out to me. He saw something in me that I wouldn't see in myself for years. Mr. Berini opened the door to the possibility that I was worthwhile by helping me obtain a scholarship for college and encouraging me to go for it.

The people whose names appear on those two lists aren't crazy or dumb. They loved you before you were old enough to question it. They love you now, the real you, even if you try to hide it. Whenever you doubt yourself or get tempted to put yourself down, think of them. Would they allow you to mistreat yourself? Would they tell you to give up, forget about it, no one will ever love you? Would you dare tell them the names you call yourself in your darkest moments? Of course not. Thinking about these people will instantly take you back to the knowledge—the *certainty*—that you are loved and worth loving. You could take it further by writing about the positive encouragement or compliments they gave you, or by recalling an especially memorable time you spent together.

I have met quite a few people who tell me that no one at all loved them when they were children. No one tucked them in, cheered them on, or taught them what love means. Their Love

History is comprised of bits and pieces—a kind gesture from a scout leader, a hug from a best friend. Some people's warmest memories are of their pets. But just because you didn't get enough love as a child doesn't mean you aren't worthy of love or that it is out of your reach forever. My own parents never attended my basketball games or watched me perform in the marching band. They didn't read me bedtime stories or ask how my day went. That doesn't make me incapable of giving and receiving love or of loving myself, it only shows me that there are different ways to love. And it reminds me that as an adult, it is ultimately my job to cultivate loving relationships around me. My parents (even my father) loved me the way they knew how. The events that happened later don't undo that love or make me unworthy. In order to move past my family legacy, I have learned to give myself the love I want rather than wait for someone else to fill me up and tell me that I'm okay.

Understanding your Love History reassures you that you are lovable, but it also supplies you with another valuable insight. It helps clarify what love means to you. A few fortunate people grow up surrounded by love that is plentiful, freely given, and unconditional, but most of us have Love Histories that tell a more complicated tale. There was love, but not without obligations. Or it never felt like enough. Or it was all mixed up with sibling rivalry. Or it came at a heavy cost, such as having to turn a blind eye to someone else's pain. Does that mean the love you experienced doesn't count? No. Love is messy. Your parents, family, and friends are not saints, and their love for you may not have been perfect, but it still counts. However, the way you experienced love when you were young does affect the way you perceive it later on in life.

There is no good or bad Love History, no letter grade or seal of approval. The important thing is that you know where you stand.

When you willingly face your past, you can let go of the wounds that have held you back from expressing the essential nature that is you. That is the first step on your way to loving fearlessly, because whether or not you realize it, your Love History has been the silent standard by which you judge new friends and lovers. It is where some of your expectations about love were born, and it may be the reason your past relationships did not feel genuine or good enough. That's all right. What matters is that now you are willing to learn new ways to love that don't precisely match what you already know.

☀ Fearbuster Exercise: ☀ What Does Love Mean to You?

Grab your journal and write down your definition of love. List a few actions you equate with being loved. It could be flowers on your birthday or being acknowledged when you walk into a room. Perhaps it is someone calling you every Sunday morning like clockwork, or offering to help you do your taxes, or cooking your favorite meal.

Next, list three or more actions you take to show someone you love him (or her). Again, they don't have to be big, flashy demonstrations. In fact, I'm more interested in the little things you do for the people you love.

Finally, write a few sentences explaining how love would show up in your everyday life if you were not afraid—today, not when you get it all together. I emphasize everyday life because when we think of love, we usually imagine special events or vacations. That's not reality. The "dailyness" of life is where love and fear meet, and where love either flourishes or fades.

History Repeats Itself:
Your Perception of Love

Did you ever hear the saying, "Those who cannot remember the past are condemned to repeat it"? Likewise, those who do not understand their Love History are condemned to repeat the same types of relationships. If you are self-aware—make that, if you are breathing—you have probably noticed blatant relationship patterns such as being attracted to blondes or being drawn to certain personality types even though you *know* they're not good for you. This sort of pattern usually has to do with sexual chemistry, which I talk about in Truth 4, "Chemistry Is Between Your Ears." Right now, I want you to think about a different kind of pattern, one that has to do with your perception of love. This perception, which has its roots in your Love History, affects all your relationships. To increase the love in your life, you need to understand how your perception of it may be limiting you. Like my client Tamara, your narrow perception of love may be causing you to repeat the same blunders in relationship after relationship.

Tamara was forty but didn't look a day over thirty-five. She greeted me with a warm smile, then settled into a corner of my sofa. She looked extremely comfy there—the act of reclining suited her.

"I know it probably doesn't seem like I should be here," she said, shaking her head regretfully. "But I can't solve this myself. I have never found a man who's a match for me in the love arena. They just can't keep up with me. The problem is, my heart is too big. I have a lot of love to give—*a lot*—and the men I meet get scared off by it. My love is too real for them. I need your help finding someone who will jump into it with me and go all the way."

"Are you sure it's the men you're meeting, and not you?" I asked her.

"Well, my friends all tell me my standards are too high, but this is my life and I feel very comfortable with my high standards."

"Then you won't mind finding out how you perceive love."

"Not at all. Bring it on."

"Great. I want to hear all about your past relationships, and your perceptions about love may shed a lot of light on those."

I asked Tamara to complete the following exercise. You might like to do the same.

Fearbuster Exercise: Your Perception of Love

Answer the following questions. Do not filter. Do not think. Do not question what comes up for you. If it seems to have nothing to do with the question, write it down anyway.

- What are your negative thoughts about_____love_____?

- How do those thoughts make you feel?

- When you have those feelings, what do you do or not do?

Why only negative thoughts? Well, positive thoughts about love probably aren't causing you any problems! It's the negative thoughts that set off a chain reaction leading to your Wheel of Fear and self-defeating behavior patterns. So complete the exercise and find out what your own pattern looks like.

If you are dating, you may want to answer those three questions using the word *dating* as well as *love*. The same goes for *marriage* or *living together* or just the word *relationships* or *commitment*. If those seem too general, you can use your mate's first name or that of an ex-lover. Answer the questions about any love-related word that pushes your buttons or that you want to avoid or deny. The negative thoughts you write down are the perceptions you carry around with you. They are the responses your fear has produced to keep you safe, yet these perceptions do not necessarily reflect reality.

I realize that you don't think this way all the time. When you are on your Wheel of Freedom, these negative thoughts have no power over you. You are able to separate reality from fiction. These thoughts are within you, but they are not you. When you are fearless, they evaporate. Being aware of them will help set you free.

Tamara's Perceptions: You Can't Trust Love

Tamara chose to write about love. I told her to jot down anything that popped into her mind and to leave no thought unturned, even if it seemed unrelated. The more truthful she was, the more fears would be revealed, giving her the information she needed to change her pattern.

What are your negative thoughts about love?

Mr. Right does not exist.

All the good men are taken.

No one wants to make a commitment anymore.

I don't trust people when they say I love you; they just want something.

Love isn't worth the effort. It always breaks your heart.

21

Love is the woman's responsibility; men only want one thing.

If you base your relationship on love, it will only disappoint you.

How do those thoughts make you feel?

Sad

Betrayed

Hurt

Angry

Frustrated

Cynical

Righteous

Depressed

When you have those feelings, what do you do?

When I feel sad, I stay home and eat chocolate-chip cookie-dough ice cream to cheer myself up.

When I feel betrayed, I isolate.

When I feel hurt, I try to get a man to notice me so I think better of myself.

When I feel angry, I lash out.

When I feel frustrated, I pick a fight.

When I feel cynical, I think everyone is stupid and lazy.

When I feel righteous, I don't listen to anyone.

When I feel depressed, I stay home and watch movie after movie.

Tamara's feelings appear to be dictating her actions, but it is her *thoughts* that produced those feelings in the first place. And many of Tamara's thoughts grew out of her fears. She fears there are no good men left. Clearly this cannot be true. Yet that thought triggers feelings of sadness and depression, and to drown out those feelings, she eats or stays home watching movies.

This Fearbuster Exercise reveals how your perceptions influence your behavior when you allow fear to be in control. We typically deal with negative, fear-based thoughts by doing something to drown out the bad feeling those thoughts bring up. It doesn't work. The only effective way to master fear, which is the root cause of our so-called bad feelings, is to take actions grounded in freedom. And those actions are very different from the actions we take to repress a fearful feeling, such as gorging ourselves or watching movies at home all day. The good news is, when we become aware of how fear colors our perceptions and influences our behavior, we can choose differently. We can choose freedom.

Fearbuster Exercise: Who Is Responsible for Love?

I now wanted Tamara to see how her negative perceptions had influenced the way she had experienced love in the past. I asked her to list her three most significant relationships and explain how they had ended, who was responsible for the outcome, and the reason the breakup occurred.

You can do the exercise, too. Select your top three relationships, and please don't claim that you were one hundred percent responsible for all the breakups or that both partners were fifty/fifty every time. You might think those are the "right" (evolved) answers, but they are not the truthful ones. Most of us end a relationship with a long list of reasons why it failed, and most of the time we don't think it's our fault. I understand that in spiritual terms it is nobody's fault, but regardless of how we rationalize it, somewhere within us we do assign blame to make sense of it all. It may not be the right thing to do, but we do it because we're human.

Name	% My Responsibility	% My Partner's Responsibility	Ending	Reason

I have had clients who didn't date anyone for longer than six months and swore they had never been in love. They were unsure about who to choose for this exercise, so I told them that a relationship qualifies if they dated the person for more than three months *and* did one or more of the following:

- Brought the person to an office party

- Introduced the person to their family

- Introduced the person to their friends

- Gave the person a gift for a significant holiday, such as Christmas, Valentine's Day, or a birthday

- Helped the person through an illness or crisis

Tamara Tells the Truth

Tamara wanted to give me the fifty/fifty answer for all her relationships, saying, "Hey, it takes two to tango. I know I'm not perfect." But when I asked her to talk about the specific reasons behind each breakup, quite a different story emerged. Here is her list.

Name	% My Responsibility	% My Partner's Responsibility	Ending	Reason
Peter:	20	80	big scene, no contact	too young, he wouldn't commit
Lou:	40	60	hung up on him	he talked about his ex
Darren:	30	70	divorced	he was a workaholic

Peter was Tamara's college sweetheart, but after dating him for eighteen months she broke it off. "I gave him an ultimatum. He wouldn't commit to marriage, so I ended it." After graduating at twenty-four she met Lou, who seemed like the ideal partner. But after six months of hearing how she was just like his ex, Tamara split, taking forty percent of the blame for staying too long. At twenty-nine she met Darren, who worked too much but told her he loved her. She liked his hard-driving style and married him after a brief courtship. Tamara's frustration started to build from the moment the honeymoon was over. In her mind, the next nine years consisted of her trying to save the marriage and Darren refusing to change. Sure, he begged her to stay, but he didn't prove he really loved her by changing in the way she had asked him to. That put Darren in the seventy-percent-his-responsibility category. They divorced.

When Tamara wrote this information down in a simple list, she was surprised at how skewed her percentages were. She took little responsibility for her breakups and had consistently seen her role as passive, focusing on how the man was not fulfilling her needs. In each relationship, her well-being had centered around how the man treated her rather than an inner sense of self-worth. Tamara waited for men to romance her, pay attention to her, or change for her. When they didn't perform to her expectations, she broke it off. Her reasons for ending a relationship always had to do with the man's inadequacies rather than her own lack of experience, imagination, or compassion.

I was not on the scene for Tamara's relationships and didn't have a clue what had actually gone on between her and these men, but that wasn't the point of the exercise. I wanted Tamara to grasp the way she perceived her role in relationships. As we talked about the exercises, it was clear to both of us that she had a tendency to blame her partner and not recognize herself as being just as influential as he was. Her Love History, which we uncovered in the weeks that followed, revealed a sense of scarcity, a fear that there wasn't enough love to go around. She played it out in her relationships, waiting for the man to live up to a vague, unattainable standard and always feeling unappreciated and badly loved. She expressed this as, "My heart is too big. I have so much love to give, no man can match me."

Everyone falls on one side of the responsibility divide or the other. Those who feel their partners are mostly to blame for the breakups—and they account for about eighty percent of the clients I work with—tend to perceive love as something that happens *to* them. In their view, love is not a verb. It is not what they do. It is what they deserve or need. Like Tamara reclining on my sofa, they are ready to "receive" love. They are willing to look for it and eager to grab at it. That's all well and fine, but half of loving—the half you control—involves giving, not receiving. It involves being loving, not telling yourself you deserve love. We are all worthy to receive love. And while Tamara insisted that she had "so much love to give," her talks with me revealed that fear had frozen her love. By denying her responsibility in the relationships, she was essentially giving away her power and making herself helpless and passive. On the positive side, as we worked together she learned to see that disappointments can also be opportunities to set boundaries, get clear on what matters most, or learn new communication skills.

What happened in Tamara's past was water under the bridge. Even if she had claimed more responsibility, her relationships might have ended. Now it was time to move forward. Tamara was asking for my help, and I knew of only one path for her. It was the one I have chosen for myself and that I offer you in this book: Understand that fear changes your perception of reality. The rest of the Truths will point the way out of your fears and teach you new ways to find more love, for yourself as well as for the people around you.

When you consciously choose freedom over fear, you will gain the courage to be loving no matter what your past relationships were like. Instead of talking about how much love you have to give, you will be able to start giving it. Be loving, and the love in your life will increase.

☀ Fearbuster Exercise: ☀ How Do I Love Me?

Each day I encourage you to list one or more ways you are showing love to yourself. Perhaps it is taking a moment out of your busy day and telling yourself you are doing a good job. Maybe it is paying attention to when you are kind even though you don't feel like it. It could be letting go of some criticism you received and not taking it personally. It may even be something as simple as giving yourself plenty of time in the morning so you don't have to rush around getting ready. I invite you to list anything at all that is helping you learn a little bit more about yourself and your ability to love.

Today, I loved myself by:

1. _____

2. _____

3. _____

4. _____

5. _____

Combining your Love History of the past and the Love History you are creating day by day will add up to a different experience of love in the future.

Your Love Legacy

Your Love History and the information from the Fearbuster Exercises in this chapter add up to what I call a Love Legacy. This is the combined effect of all the people who taught you how to love and those you loved in return. It includes the relationships that worked and those that didn't. Your Love Legacy shows you where you are right now in terms of your perceived capacity to be loving. It is your starting point for future relationships. As you become willing to uncover your fears, you will see how your Love Legacy is influencing your feelings and choices. At that moment, you are poised for a new beginning. You will know where you stand, and you can use that awareness to help you choose who to befriend, who to keep at arm's length, who to draw close, who to let in, who to love.

A Birthday Wish

My fortieth birthday was a monumental one for me. My mother was murdered when she was only thirty-nine, which meant that from now on I would see days she never got the opportunity to see. Just like her, when I was thirty-nine I went through some major transitions. I enlarged my vision for my life. I altered my view of my relationships. I claimed my power and increased my self-esteem. I wrote and published *Fearless Living*. As I looked back, I could see that my whole life had been leading up to this moment, when the world would show itself to be a loving and promising place full of opportunities.

Turning forty, I stepped back and took stock of all I had created. Everything that had gone before made sense, even the events I had always thought of as false starts, mistakes, or bad choices. Being a waitress had taught me how to run a business, read people, and be friendly no matter what. It showed me how to be of service. When I was in marketing and public relations I learned how to speak powerfully and find the nugget of wisdom within the message. During my depression, I learned how to surrender and trust. And when I attempted suicide, I learned that life is precious and people can't help you change unless you are willing to look at things differently.

When my mother celebrated her thirty-ninth birthday, I remember thinking of her as old and a little chunky. Now that I am passing her in age I look at my body and notice it is identical to hers, yet I feel neither old nor chunky. My mother and I have other things in common. People have told me she was always smiling, enthusiastic, and filled with positive energy. They have said the same things about me, and I'm thankful I inherited those traits. Yet despite our similarities, my mother and I are different in one crucial way. I have gotten to live long enough to realize that I am not my fears. I can reinvent myself. She didn't get that chance.

You have the chance. You don't have to wait until you are fully healed or one hundred percent fearless or completely prepared for love. Love is messy and always will be, but love is there for you. Now, today, this moment. You are right on time.

Truth 2

Everyone Is Innocent

"I can't stand show-offs," my friend Karen grumbled as we finished up a morning walk. Our route had taken us past one of those health clubs where the treadmills face the street through a bank of floor-to-ceiling windows. Men and women in wisps of workout gear toiled silently behind the glass, sweating in a way that made them glow rather than drip. No doubt about it, their physiques were stunning.

"What kind of person wants to work out in front of a window, anyway?" Karen continued. "Unless the point is to make us normal-bodied people feel even fatter and guiltier than we already do."

"Your fears are showing," I teased her.

"Oh, Rhonda, please. You have to agree with me this time. People only exercise in front of those windows so they can show off their bods."

"Not so they can look outside? Maybe they're tired of watching TV. You have no evidence they're showing off. In fact, let's take it a little further. What if one of the guys in there asks you out some day? Are you going to turn him down because you saw him working out in this window and he must be a show-off?"

"Okay, I get your point," she laughed. "I didn't think about it that way."

"I understand. I used to do it, too."

"Do what?"

"Assume that it's me against the world. That everyone is guilty until proven innocent. It's how you feel when fear is your default position."

"What do you mean?"

"We tend to go through life braced for the worst. Even if something has no positive or negative attached to it, like people working out in a window, we take it personally and get defensive. Fear becomes our default position."

"Not me," said Karen. "I'm a very loving person. You'd have to work pretty hard to convince me my default is fear."

Never one to sidestep a challenge, I went home that day and thought about what Karen had said. I believe most of us do perceive the world from a fearful place, we just don't realize it. Like Karen, we consider ourselves loving and open-minded. But fear doesn't always stand up and announce itself. It usually operates under our conscious radar. Our fear exists to protect us, but when fear is the default—when we automatically assume the worst—it stifles our ability to love other people, accept their love, and be open to the love around us.

The fear default is so ingrained that we aren't aware of how we use it to judge people's motives. Karen had asked me to prove it to her, so I came up with a little game. You can try it, too. Write down the very first feeling you have—one word only—when you read the following statements.

- You're eating at a restaurant and your boyfriend watches an attractive woman walk past your table.

- Your fiancé buys a new sofa without asking your opinion of it.

- You buy your wife a present and she asks if you've kept the receipt.

- You meet your mother for lunch and the first thing she says is, "You changed your hair."

- Your husband gives you a teddy for your anniversary. It is two sizes too small.

- Your co-worker offers to fix you up on a blind date with her ex-boyfriend.

- Your father points out that your latest love doesn't have a *real* job.

- Your support group forgets your birthday.

- Your mother asks if you're dating anyone yet.

- Your girlfriend says that before you meet her parents, she'd like to take you clothes shopping.

- As your boyfriend is kissing you he whispers, "I love your laugh lines."

Now, look at your reactions and consider the following possibilities. What if your husband really thinks you wear a size six? What if your mother actually likes your haircut? What if your co-worker's ex would be a perfect match for you? What if it never occurred to your fiancé that you would care about the sofa? What if no one is using you, testing you, or undermining you? What if the people who offended you don't even realize it? What if it is not you against the world?

What if everyone is innocent?

I know, I know. It goes against everything we've been taught. Early on, we learn to question, doubt, and be on the lookout for users. We place great value on defending ourselves, being right, and keeping it together at all costs. We don't see this as fearful, we see it as streetwise and reasonable.

I disagree.

I believe that choosing to treat people as if they are innocent is the very foundation of learning to love fearlessly. It isn't about being naive or a wimp. It isn't about ignoring your hunches or finding an excuse to stay with someone who treats you badly. Seeing people as innocent is simply an approach to life that works better than being afraid and defensive. Not only is it more loving, it's more realistic. Because ninety-nine percent of the time, other people are not out to get you. They're not even thinking about you. Most of them are operating from fear, and their first goal is to protect themselves. They're just trying to stay safe and maybe get a little love along the way.

What happens when you assume people are arrogant, incompetent, or otherwise flawed? They pick up on it immediately and steel themselves for an attack. They isolate, not wanting to expose themselves to potential pain. They ignore you in an effort to put you in your place. And it all occurs in a split second. Fear is the basis for most people's behavior, and when you realize that, you begin to grasp the enormous power of your own attitude. You can't change other people's fears, but by treating them as if they are innocent you can profoundly change the dynamics of your relationship.

When you refuse to put people into boxes—conceited, unhelpful, dumb—and instead are willing to believe they might surprise you, you are seeing them as innocent. When you resist profiling people based on their past behavior and approach them as if anything is possible, you are seeing them as innocent. When you smile first; when you give them a break; when you take their comments at face value; when you assume they are doing their best; when you explain it twice without sighing; when you stop taking things so personally; when you accept a compliment without wondering about ulterior motives, you are seeing people as innocent. And seeing people as innocent is the greatest gift you can give another human being: the gift of acceptance.

Some people are not innocent. I realize that. But did you realize that when you make a practice of seeing everyone as innocent, it becomes much easier to recognize the ones who are not? As you approach the world with your eyes and heart open—listening, paying attention, really seeing other people—you will develop the skill to discern who is in fear and who is using fear against you. When you no longer see darkness and deception where it doesn't exist, the real thing is much easier to spot. People with bad intentions will stick out like a sore thumb.

How would your life be different if other people saw *you* as innocent? Would it be easier to change? Would it be easier to forgive yourself for your past? Would it be easier to love yourself and others? Would it be easier to be you? You can have all that by going first. That is the gift of seeing everyone as innocent. No more hidden agendas. No more assumptions. No more making things up to prove your point. No more building evidence to keep love out. It is a seismic shift in perception, but it can be done.

The Earth Moves

Several years ago I made a conscious choice to treat everyone I met as if he or she were innocent. It all started with my roommate, Lucy. I had recently moved in with her, and being new to town, I asked her to recommend a hairdresser. I noticed she got tons of compliments and figured her hair guru could work his magic on me, too. I made an appointment immediately. Anticipating my great new look, I also made a date for the evening. A blind date.

As Mr. Guru was drying my hair, I got a glimpse of myself in the mirror. It was awful. My blonde hair had turned into an orange ball of ugly. I was shattered. I had never looked this bad, and it was all because of this idiot and Lucy, who had steered me to him. Crying, I started to give him a piece of my mind. "How dare you ruin my hair! What were you thinking with this color? Are you using me as a guinea pig for a new product? I can't believe how incompetent you are!" I stormed out, certain he was a terrible hairdresser. Back at the apartment, I phoned my date and cancelled, telling him I was sick. I was sick all right. Sick of being pushed around by incompetent people.

The following day, still upset, I caught Lucy as she was walking out the door. When I asked her where she was going, she replied, "To get my hair done." How could she? What kind of friend would continue to see someone who purposely ruined my hair?

"Look what he did to me, Lucy!" I protested.

She calmly looked me in the eye and said, "But he does a great job on me."

I was speechless and she was right. He did do a great job on her hair. It was one of those moments when insight strikes you out of the blue. What if he had tried to do a great job on mine as well, and was just as upset about the results as I was? What if he was fretting about it this very minute? What would have happened if I had let him get a few words in? How could things have been different? Maybe he wasn't a horrid man after all. And I wanted to believe

Lucy hadn't purposely planned my demise. She had been a good friend on every other occasion. I was the one who had put Mr. Guru on trial and convinced myself of his guilt, as well as Lucy's. What kind of person was I to do such a thing? A person in fear. Working on the Fearless Living program, I had begun to understand how my fears were clouding my perceptions. The information I received was being filtered either through my fears or through my commitment to freedom. I now knew that I had a choice.

Over the next few weeks, I went through a period of deep reflection about my past relationships, not just with men but with everyone. What I saw didn't make me very happy. I had no long-term friends, just a bunch of people I thought had betrayed me. What if they hadn't? What if I had done the same to them as I was about to do to Lucy? What if *I* was the reason I had no long-term friends? And then it hit me. If I couldn't maintain friendships, no wonder I couldn't find love. My most cherished evidence about the world—that people would find out I was a loser and abandon me— had made fear my natural reaction. When things went wrong, my fear kicked in and I ended up with the situation I now found myself in with Lucy. Even when people (especially men) were nice, I suspected their motives. It was inconceivable that anyone would like the real me.

I forced myself to sit down and take my fear-based assumptions to their furthest conclusion. If I assumed everyone was out to get me, I would have to be vigilant about defending myself every moment of my life. I would constantly be trying to figure out what other people wanted from me. Were they after my knowledge, my connections, my time, my money, my body, my love? It would be exhausting and I would never be able to go into a situation with an open heart. I would have to stay guarded until people earned my trust by proving that all they wanted was to know the real me.

But people don't work that hard to get to know someone. If I always put up barriers, why would anyone even bother to ask me out for a cup of coffee? How would I make any friends? How would I find love? And besides, where was my proof that they had a hidden agenda?

I asked myself whether I did all the plotting and maneuvering I assumed other people were doing. Was I a manipulator? Did I hide my motives to gain a minor edge? Did I exploit my friends, undermine my co-workers, and only call someone when I needed a favor? No, I didn't. I'm not saying I was a saint. I had my less-than-noble moments, my vengeful thoughts, my get-even fantasies. But mostly I played fair and meant well. I may have been fearful, but I was innocent.

I decided that from that day forward I would see everyone as innocent. Myself. Lucy. Even the hairdresser. (I called and apologized for my outburst, but I didn't let him touch my hair again!) I had no idea how this innocence thing would play out, but I knew I had nothing to lose and everything to gain.

I made a commitment to take the focus off myself. I resisted the urge to take everything personally, and began treating others as kindly as I could, no matter how I was feeling. I would no longer make up stories about the actions they took, the words they said, or why they could never love me. Instead, I would listen as if they were telling me the truth, ask questions when I didn't understand, and allow others the room to have their feelings instead of making it all about me. No more assigning hidden motives, prejudging, and cutting people off before I separated fact from fiction. I would practice seeing the best in everyone by connecting with them instead of defending myself. I would steadfastly remind myself that people weren't out to use me. They were just afraid.

You Can't Get Stepped On If You're Not Lying Down

"But Rhonda," said my boyfriend-of-the-month when I told him of this revelation, "You're leaving yourself wide open! It's a fact of life that some people are nice to you only because they want something. If you see everyone as innocent, people are going to use you."

That was a tough one. I had thought about it long and hard before I came to a startlingly simple conclusion. "Yes, some people might be nice only because they want something from me. So what? It doesn't mean I have to give it to them." I realized I had a choice. If someone was kind, I could choose to enjoy the kindness, say thank you, and walk away feeling valued but not exploited. Seeing other people as innocent means you are willing to believe they have good intentions, not covert ones. It means you can accept a kindness graciously without feeling obligated to return it.

When someone goes out of his way for you, do you instantly feel responsible for his actions? That is fear. Fear of hurting his feelings. Fear of being seen as mean or selfish, even though you never asked for the kindness. Fear of saying, "No thank you," even if that would be the truth. It doesn't occur to most of us to accept a kindness as just that, a kindness. Instead, kindness usually activates our Wheel of Fear and we start worrying about being obligated.

How often do you second-guess people who are nice to you? *I wonder why Tom gave me that compliment . . . I wonder why Sarah was so friendly this morning . . . I wonder why Keith left that can of soda on my desk. . . .* We don't wonder, we know! *Tom wants me to work overtime for him tonight. Sarah needs me to baby-sit the kids. Keith is hinting around for some of that candy I got last week.* We're convinced we can read the minds of our friends, strangers, and anyone else who happens to cross our path. In truth, we never really know what motivates other people. We can guess, and occasionally we might even be right, but the only way we can be sure is if we ask them.

That's what I do. I have actually been known to say, "Gee, why are you being so nice to me? I love it! But is there something you need?" I've got a pretty good instinct about these things, and sometimes the other person will say, "As a matter of fact, there *is* a favor I wanted to ask you." I listen to them, and then I decide whether or not I want to do it. Treating people as if they are innocent doesn't mean being a doormat. It doesn't mean you have to give everyone what they want. Their asking is only uncomfortable if you can't say no. (In Truth 6, you will learn when and how to say no.)

And what about people who aren't innocent at all, and don't pretend to be? What about the rude sales clerk, the co-worker who actually *is* backstabbing you, the ex-boyfriend who is going around bad-mouthing you, the boss who takes credit for your work? Of course these people exist, and seeing everyone as innocent won't make them disappear. Fortunately, most of us don't deal with more than one or two of them at a time. (If you feel that you're surrounded by traitors and slackers, I urge you to take a close look at yourself, as I did. Your perceptions might be off.)

The thing to remember about people who behave badly is that they are in fear. That fact will be very obvious to you, if you are coming from freedom. When you assume people are innocent, you give them the benefit of the doubt *until they prove you wrong*. At that point, your goal is to stand up for yourself, see them clearly, and detach. Do not take their actions personally, because even if the actions are intended to harm you, it's not really about you. It's about their own fear.

The rude sales clerk could have a million fears behind her nasty attitude, none of them having to do with you. People who backstab their co-workers are usually afraid they aren't smart enough for the job; they believe they must push others down to get an edge. Your bad-mouthing ex? Afraid his buddies will think he's a loser for losing you. Your credit-stealing boss? Afraid his work can't stand on its own. None of these fears excuses their behavior, but when you recognize that fear—not hostility toward you—is behind that behavior, it changes the way you percieve their actions. Instead of backing off or getting hostile in return, you straighten your shoulders and remember who you are. And you set boundaries. (I'll show you how in Truth 6.)

I Can See Clearly Now

When I started treating people as if they were innocent, I was astonished at the power of it. It changed my experience of the world dramatically. In the beginning I didn't really believe everyone was innocent, I just behaved *as if* I believed they were. It didn't matter. I got the same positive results. You will too, and you don't have to believe it either. Just go through the motions and let this truth reveal itself to you.

What happens when you start behaving as if everyone is innocent? You get lighter because you are no longer carrying around the weight of all those suspicions. You're not distracted by second-guessing everyone's motives, so your concentration improves. You perceive things more clearly because you are in the moment—listening, thinking, and responding to what the other person is saying right now. People surprise you because you allow them to be different than they've been before. You can stop constructing inner dialogues for confrontations that never take place. You don't have to figure out all the ways people might try to manipulate or use you. You don't have to take them home with you. You can quit protecting yourself and accept the love they have to give.

If the thought of seeing the whole world as innocent is too much to handle all at once, go in one toe at a time. Practice on strangers and co-workers, then move on to your friends, and finally take the plunge and try seeing your boyfriend, girlfriend, or spouse as innocent. It won't happen overnight, but the benefits are well worth it. Only after I began to treat people as if they were innocent did I realize how clouded my perceptions had been in the past. Love was all around me, now that I knew how to see it.

Before my conversion to innocence, I was blinded by my own fear and never knew that my impressions of people were often wrong. In innocent mode, I forced myself to listen supportively to what the other person was saying and not to interrupt. I can't tell you how often they were coming from a place I hadn't expected. Pre-innocent days, I thought my sister Cindy only kept in touch with me because I was her sister. I was sure she didn't like me and invited me over for the holidays out of obligation. That Christmas, I decided to see Cindy and myself as innocent. As we sat together in her kitchen the night I arrived, I listened to her, asked questions about her life, and thanked her for the invite. Up until that year I had never thanked Cindy for our annual Christmas gatherings because I thought she was only doing it because she felt she had to. Why thank her for that?

Before we said good night, Cindy asked me to go Christmas shopping with her the following day. She had never done that before. We hit all the stores and I again reminded myself to see my sister as innocent. I made jokes and gave suggestions that, in the past, I would have withheld for fear she would think I was stupid or childish. And you know what? We laughed. We laughed so hard that we were no longer just sisters, we became friends. To this day, one of our favorite things to do together is holiday shopping. That year not only did I allow myself to be myself, I noticed that Cindy was a lot more relaxed, too. She saw that I was behaving differently toward her and it gave her room to let down her hair and step away from the big-sister role. We were finally getting to know each other as people, and I found out how funny and generous she really is.

Months passed, and I kept my vow to act as if others were innocent. After about a year, I had to admit it: most of the time, they really *were* innocent. Underneath their queries, opinions, and comments, they just wanted to connect and be loved. When they acted less than loving, it usually meant they were afraid. I learned to look behind their fears to their innocence, and it gave me the freedom to love them without expecting love back. When my need for proof went out the window, love was all that was left.

For me, seeing people as innocent is an everyday activity. I'm working on making innocence my default position, but it may never be as automatic as the fear response, so I have to stay vigilant. I never know when fear might try to fool me into seeing the innocent as guilty.

As I'm writing this chapter, I have just begun dating someone new, a man I'm really excited about. One afternoon a few weeks ago, he called and mentioned that he might stop by later that evening. *Stop by?* I thought to myself. *You mean, like you'd stop by a 7-Eleven? Am I just a convenience?* Red lights were flashing as I planned my defense. If he thought I was convenient, it was time to up the stakes a little bit. I was gonna make him prove he loved me. He would have to crawl through glass and break down doors to get my attention now, because I was not going to be taken for granted, not by anyone—

Just as my Wheel of Fear was rising like a circular saw, ready to slice up all the good feelings between me and my guy, I came to my senses. Why was I making stuff up about him? Why was I making him guilty? Maybe it was because I felt unsure of his feelings for me. Maybe I should just call him up and ask him why he wanted to come over. Maybe instead of waiting for him to prove his love, I should request it.

"Hi. It's me. Um, I just wanted to know, do you want to come over because you really want to be with me? Do you miss me?"

"Yes!" he said, clearly relieved. "But you sounded so strange when we talked, I wasn't going to come. I'm dying to be with you."

"Me too," I said. "Get your butt over here."

You can't remind yourself too often: Assume they are innocent. Give them the chance to love you.

What Do You Expect?

The first step in seeing people as innocent is to eliminate expectations. We all have expectations—conscious or unconscious—about life and other people. In *Fearless Living* I devoted an entire chapter to showing how you can detach from your expectations and instead begin to live with intention. This is fundamental to both living and loving fearlessly.

Let's define expectations. Expectations are what we think *should* happen as a result of our actions, words, or feelings. It is the stuff we make up about a person, place, or situation in order to validate our beliefs about the world. We call these expectations *life*, *truth*, or *the way it is*. Expectations guarantee lost moments, lost love, and lost lives. In relationships, expectations lead us to have rigid, premeditated ideas about how the other person should behave. When we expect, we are setting up our loved ones to fail and ourselves to get hurt. Disappointment is always the result.

Our expectations stem from our upbringing, belief system, and life experiences, as well as the media we're exposed to—books, music, TV, film. They are also based on hearsay, in other words, what our friends tell us about their relationships. I recall sitting with a group of women and hearing the tale of a mutual friend who had remarried at the age of forty-two and was getting the royal romantic treatment from her new husband. "He left her a note hanging from a balloon in the hallway. It just said 'I love you,' " relayed one woman with a sigh. "No one has ever done that for me."

"My husband leaves me notes all the time," piped up another woman. "The last one said, 'Pick up milk.' " Everyone laughed, but there was a wistful undertone to it. I'd bet that ninety-five percent more women get "Pick up milk" notes than floating "I love you's," and I couldn't help feeling a little sorry for the husbands of the women in that room. They would never know they were up against Casanova, and let's face it, they could never win. Little nuggets of information like this, combined with all the other data we've collected over the course of our lives, feed the expectations we place on those we love and ourselves.

Expectations filter the information we receive with one sole purpose: to validate our feelings. Fear likes to be right, and expectations are the key to perpetuating our beliefs about the world. If we grew up with an abundance of acceptance and love, perhaps we see the world through a filter called "There is plenty of love to go around." But if you are like me and love seemed scarce, you might think, "Love is hard to find." Expectations have tremendous power over our lives because they program us to repeat the past, to see only what we have seen before, and to block out new information that doesn't fit what we already believe.

Expectations can choke the love out of a relationship, but what's worse is that most of the time we neglect to tell the other person what we expect. I call this a silent contract. For instance, maybe your mother always gave you sweets when you were feeling blue. It became a silent contract between the two of you—if you glumly said, "I sure would love some brownies," that was her cue to give you not just brownies but a little extra attention. Fast forward twenty years. You mention to your girlfriend that some brownies sure would taste good about now, and she replies, "Those are loaded with fat and calories! I thought you said you wanted to lose a few pounds. Come on, let's go for a jog." You don't want an exercise plan, you want some love. But if you have to come right out and tell her you're feeling down, you'll be vulnerable. She might think you're weak or high-maintenance. Too risky! Much safer to see how well she can pick up your cues. If she really cared, she'd pay attention, right? Wrong. She is innocent of your past, she doesn't know about the silent contract between you and your mother, and she certainly doesn't know that she, too, is expected to abide by that contract.

To look at the way expectations and silent contracts have affected your own relationships, I invite you to open the memory file labeled *gifts*. Remember all those gifts you have given or received that ended up with both people being disappointed or hurt?

Take my younger sister, Linda. On her first married Christmas, the rest of the family couldn't wait to see what her new husband was going to give her. While they were courting, Joel was Mr. Romance, so now we were holding our collective breath to see what he had in store for his new bride. As she tore open the gift my heart sank. He had given her a set of knives! We were dumbstruck. Our shock only deepened when Linda thanked Joel with a kiss and said, "They're perfect!"

I couldn't wait to pull her aside and ask what the heck was going on. "Have you turned into a hausfrau after only a year? Wouldn't you have liked something a little more romantic?"

Thank goodness Linda was way ahead of me in seeing people as innocent. She told me that she had casually mentioned to Joel that she needed a new set of knives. "I guess he thought I really wanted them badly," she laughed. "Next time I better be more careful what I ask for."

I know from client coaching that very few people are as level-headed as Linda when it comes to gifts. On the contrary, most are fiercely attached to gifts and their supposed significance. I have asked my clients, male and female, what would make the perfect gift, and here is what they've told me. The ideal gift must be:

- A surprise

- Something the person has hinted at but not specifically requested

- *Not* something that the giver wants; something only the recipient wants

- Something that strains the budget or is handmade by the giver

- Something that reminds the receiver of a special time

- A flattering color and style

- The right size

- Unusual or one-of-a-kind

How can anyone successfully navigate this minefield? It's a shame that a well-meaning, innocent gesture such as a gift so often becomes weighed down with all those expectations. An opportunity to feel loved and to express love, lost! What if, instead of using gifts as the ultimate barometer of love, you viewed them as frosting on the cake? What if instead of getting all keyed up about whether the gift you receive is good enough, you made sure to watch the expression on the other person's face as you opened it? Most of the time, that expression is one of nervous excitement—you can see how badly they want to please you. And what if, instead of worrying about how unforgettable your gift will be, you trusted that the other person will like it simply because it's from you? With no expectations, you can enjoy whatever you receive and feel fine about whatever you give.

I mention all this to show you how expectation is different than intention. Expectation sets you up to be disappointed, while intention frees you to focus on the moment. When you expect, you are in waiting mode, hoping others will perform just the right moves to make you feel loved. In intention, you are proactive and accountable for your own love quota. When you expect, you do all the thinking and deciding by yourself. There is no connection. Instead, guilt and insecurity lead the way, and no one wins. But when you live with intention, you know you are not alone in any relationship. Conversations are not tests, they are opportunities to express love. When you approach your relationships with intention instead of expectation, you and your partner will both feel loved, appreciated, and sometimes vulnerable. That is what innocence feels like.

Intention Explained

Intention is a cornerstone of *Fearless Loving*, but what exactly does it mean? The definition I wrote in *Fearless Living* is worth repeating here: "Intention is living purposefully. On purpose, with purpose. Proactively, responsibly, and intuitively. When we intend, we erase 'should' from our vocabulary. Intention is living in the present and actively choosing the future while being aware that in each moment, your state of mind is up to you."

Intention focuses on the present moment because people and situations can change. Personal accountability is paramount, which means your life is in your hands. If you don't feel loved, you ask yourself whether you are willing to see the love. If you don't know how to love, you take responsibility and practice loving actions, loving words, and being in a place of love regardless of what the rest of the world is doing. If you don't know how to find love with a significant other, you don't blame the circumstances of life. Instead you brainstorm, ask for help, and are willing to be wrong about your ideas about love. Intention is about being here now, being loving no matter who you are with, and seeing that love is the essence of freedom. When love is in your hands, when you are in charge of your loving attitude, love just seems to surround you effortlessly. That is loving with intention. It relies on no one else.

How do intention and expectation play out in real life? Let's say you've been dating Tom for six months and he asks you out for New Year's Eve. If you are coming from a place of expectation, you might think, "Since we've been dating for six months, I expect him to make it a really special evening." Six months is an unspoken benchmark for dating couples, a nationwide silent contract, if you will. I happen to know that women view it very differently than men do. A lot of men are nervous about the six-month mark because they believe women are expecting them to make a commitment at that point, and they resent being bullied by what they view as an arbitrary deadline. Six-month expectations and the showdowns that go along with them can be very bad news.

If you rely on expectations, you are not in control of your own feelings. Either Tom will live up to your expectations and "make the evening special" or he won't, which gives him power over your mood. But you have a choice. You can approach the evening with intention instead of expectation and say to yourself, "I intend to spend New Year's Eve with Tom and celebrate the fact that I'm still crazy about him after six months. No matter where we go or what we do, I intend to enjoy myself."

You are in control of your intentions—they have nothing to do with the people you are with, the places you go, or the situations you find yourself in. Unless Tom pulls a Mr. Hyde and becomes someone totally different, there is no reason why the two of you couldn't enjoy yourselves on New Year's Eve if that's what you intend to do. (And if he did become Mr. Hyde, it would only give you an opportunity to practice seeing him as innocent.) Intention frees you to love fully, all the way to your limits, without depending on someone else for validation.

Intentional Loving: The Play Book

Loving with intention doesn't come naturally. You have to think about it and practice it. When you do, you will find your worries, expectations, and judgments falling away, and you'll be exactly where you need to be for love to thrive: in the present moment.

People who are dating sometimes have a better chance of loving with intention than people in steady relationships. They are starting fresh, whereas established couples can have a backlog of silent contracts and relationship baggage that can get in the way of random acts of love. I wanted to help established couples overcome their hesitation about loving with intention and came up with a tool that is simple but amazingly effective. I call it the Play Book.

Here's how it works. You begin with a blank book. In this book, both you and your partner write down all the ways you would like to have fun together. You share your secret desires and guilty or silly pleasures. I suggest the following categories:

- Gifts I would like to receive

- Favorite restaurants

- Places I would like to vacation

- Weekend trips I would like to take

- A dream day together would be:

- If we had two hours free, I would like to:

- If we had half a day together, I would like to:

Too often, couples become afraid to step out of the familiar routine because every decision, whether it's about a vacation, a restaurant, or even a video rental, is potentially explosive. You don't want to disappoint the other person or be blamed for choosing incorrectly, so you stick to what you know and then complain that everything feels stale. The Play Book takes the angst out of your fun time together. When you fill in those pages, you are saying that love is something more than psychic talent. You're letting your mate know that you want both of you to be happy. You are showing that you have no ulterior motives, such as setting him or her up to fail at pleasing you so you can feel victimized or superior.

Does writing down these desires take away the surprise? Not

according to the couples who have tried it. For most people, it's a chance to put forth ideas that never would have seen the light of day if it weren't for the Play Book. In part this is because we tend to forget about restaurants, movies, and so forth if we don't write them down. As for guilty pleasures, it may be easier to write that you'd like to make love in the backyard in the middle of the afternoon than to say it out loud.

Newlyweds Julie, thirty-three, and Fred, thirty-five, were afraid of getting into a routine but felt powerless to stop it. Each night they arrived home from their jobs too hungry to think and too tired to cook. They ended up at the same restaurant eating the same thing at least three nights a week. Even though they had promised as part of their wedding vows to keep their romance alive, their weekly "date night" had also fallen by the wayside. Their love life was beginning to mirror their eating habits. They didn't like it.

I told Fred about the Play Book and said that for immediate results he might want to focus on restaurants that were within two miles of their home. I encouraged him to e-mail his friends for suggestions, look at reviews in his local paper, and notice different restaurants as he was driving around. Within a week, he had jotted down five new restaurants.

"Use the Play Book to do your thinking for you," I said. "When you come home exhausted, instead of racking your brain for something different, look up a restaurant and go. Ask Julie to do the same. This is one way to show your commitment to love with intention."

A month later Fred called and gave me the good news: He and Julie were beginning to show signs of recovery.

"It was my turn to plan the date night but I got home late and was beginning to panic. So I decided to look through Julie's list in our Play Book. The difference was amazing. For the first time, I had no stress, because I knew what Julie wanted to do. The information was all right there. We went out to a new restaurant and actually had fun. Julie and I had more space to enjoy each other instead of blaming each other for that stuck-in-the-rut feeling."

The Play Book will transform your time together. All you have to do is fill in the categories. If you are in a relationship, try it. Stop making love a contest or a game. Make it easy. Make it fun. Take responsibility. Keep the book out in plain view as a reminder that your love is worth the extra effort. Add to it as you find new areas of interest, and change it as your tastes evolve. It's a wonderful way to keep your love alive, and just as important, it helps your partner discover who you are. The Play Book helps you stay focused on your intention to love rather than expecting love to disappoint you one more time.

The Four Steps to Innocent Communication

Intention is an approach to the world, an attitude you bring to your life experiences. Although it may take some getting used to, in theory it is easy to understand. Sooner or later, though, most of my clients have a more pressing question. How do they practice intention with other people? What words do they say? What does communication between two "innocent" people actually sound like?

It begins when you're willing to let go of what you think should transpire (expectations) and instead allow the conversation to unfold while keeping an open mind (intention). You have to stay present, keep alert, and listen carefully. When you hurry through a conversation to get to your part or because you think you already know what the other person is going to say, you're not in the present. When you appear to be listening but are actually thinking, deciding, and judging, you can't really connect.

Innocent conversation isn't always easy or comfortable. Your feelings could show up. You might get nervous not knowing what the other person will say. Maybe you'll feel stupid or slow. Maybe you're afraid you'll be rejected. Maybe you'll feel vulnerable and exposed. Maybe when you were growing up you were never heard. Maybe nobody valued your thoughts and ideas. Maybe nobody cared. For all these reasons and so many more, your fear of being not good enough may rear its head, attempting to protect you from danger. To keep it down, you must consciously change the way you speak and listen so that your conversations will reflect your essential nature and not your Wheel of Fear.

To help you do this, I have broken down the elements of conversation into the Four Steps to Innocent Communication. When I coach couples, one of the first things we discuss is the way language affects their perceptions and influences their feelings. Bottom line: Our fears show up and are perpetuated by our language. That is true for all relationships, not just romantic ones. As I take you through the four steps, I'll use my client Glen as an example of what to do and what to avoid.

Step One: Be Responsible

The way in which you receive or deliver information is your responsibility. We all have filtering systems that delete or deny information that is not in alignment with our present beliefs. If you don't feel heard or understood, maybe it's because of your filtering system—your behavior, language, or style of listening. Perhaps you have unrealistic expectations of how others should respond to you. That is something you must be willing to change, even though your fears will always tell you it is the other person's fault. And, yes, when you are responsible you must also be willing to be vulnerable.

Glen, a sales manager for a group of automotive magazines, had been dating Jessica, a documentary film producer, for about three months. Glen came to see me when he and Jessica broke up. It happened right after Thanksgiving, which the couple had spent in Santa Barbara at the home of Glen's parents. Everyone agreed that the four-day weekend had been a big success, and Glen was thrilled with how well Jessica got along with his family. He had hoped they could spend Christmas there, too.

They had just begun the two-hour drive back to Los Angeles when Jessica "dropped the bomb," as Glen put it. "We're sitting there happy as clams and then, out of nowhere, she says, 'I need to tell you something. I got a job offer in Washington, D.C., and I've decided to take it. I'm moving next month.' I was in shock. I just couldn't believe what was coming out of her mouth. We spent the next two hours in a knock-down-drag-out fight that got really brutal. When we got home I dropped her off and told her to get lost, move, do whatever the hell she was going to do but leave me out of it."

"Back up a minute," I said. "What exactly made you so angry about this conversation?"

Glen shot me a withering look. In a mock-patient, condescending tone that might have really irritated me if I hadn't known that deep down he was innocent, he spelled out his objections. "She agrees to come meet my parents and stay with them for four days, all the while knowing that she's not coming into my life, she's about to leave it. Instead of telling me about the move before the weekend or even sometime during it, she waits until it's over. It will be incredibly humiliating to tell my mom and dad that she's moving, not to mention all the friends who knew I was getting serious about her. And how could she decide to move without at least asking my opinion first? Obviously I mean nothing to her, she's just a user and a fake."

"Had you told Jessica you were getting serious about her?"

"I invited her to my parents' house for Thanksgiving weekend. If that's not a clear sign, I don't know what is."

In his version of the conversation, Glen was innocent and Jessica was guilty of leading him on, being callous, and using him. What would have happened if Glen hadn't immediately gone on the defensive? If he had trusted Jessica even though her news was perhaps ill-timed and terribly disappointing? If he had remained calm and quietly asked about her decision? What if his words were guided by her innocence? What if he was willing to be vulnerable instead of making her decision all about him? What if he was able to see that fear was standing in their way?

In every conversation, especially the difficult ones, it is crucial that we take responsibility for the way we give and receive information. I could tell that in his anger, Glen had filtered out any information he received from Jessica about her priorities, goals, or fears. He never asked how her move would affect their relationship or how she came to the conclusion that Washington, D.C., was best. He had expectations instead, and a silent contract with Jessica that he based on her having accepted his Thanksgiving invitation. Perhaps these expectations were not realistic. Glen felt humiliated because he had told his friends he was getting serious about Jessica, but apparently he had not yet told *her* how he felt. During their conversation he could rightfully point out the things he had done to show his feelings for her, such as inviting her to meet his parents, but he also needed to acknowledge the things he had left unsaid.

Ask yourself:

Who are you blaming for the present state of your relationship?

Who are you refusing to see as innocent?

Step Two: Give Yourself and Others a Break

If you choose to believe that everyone is innocent, you will approach each conversation with the attitude that we are all doing the best we can. In the three months Glen had been dating Jessica, he had time to gauge her character. Was it likely that she had been deceiving him all along, that she cared nothing for him but went to meet his parents because she wanted to eat turkey and soak up some holiday spirit? It didn't make sense. Glen's job during their conversation was to listen and find out what was really going on with her. Even though he was hurt and angry, Glen owed it to Jessica to assume she was innocent. They had only been dating a short while, and maybe she hadn't picked up on his cues. Maybe he had missed some of hers.

"I'm going to put a few suggestions in front of you," I said. "You can decide if they have any merit. What if Jessica was too scared to tell you about her plans before this? What if dropping the bomb, as you call it, was her fear-based way of seeing if you cared? What if this move would catapult her in her career? What if she really wants you to move, too? What if she didn't tell you before because she thought that was the considerate thing to do, so the weekend wouldn't be about your relationship but about spending time with your parents? What if she didn't have the skills to tell you any other way? What if her leaving has nothing to do with you and everything to do with her?"

Glen's shoulders sagged and he looked out the window for a few moments, letting it all sink in. "I never thought of it like that," he finally said. "I just figured Jessica is a smart girl, and if she didn't mean to hurt me she wouldn't have. I felt conned and lied to. But maybe I was wrong. Do you think I've blown it with her for good?"

"No, it isn't too late. Your relationship isn't over. And now that I've given you a little tough love, here's the good news: You ought to give yourself a break, too. You did the best you could with the information and tools you had. So did Jessica. It's nothing to beat yourself up for, it's just an opportunity to see that new skills are needed. If you're willing, I can teach you some skills that will stop the two of you from destroying your love, because right now, fear is deciding your future together."

In every conversation, give yourself and others a break. Allow them the room to make mistakes, explain themselves, back up and retrace their steps if they need to. When someone is "too slow," "too stupid," or "too indecisive," give him or her a break. It's an opportunity for you to practice patience and listening. When someone is "too fast," "too complex," or "too smart," give yourself a break. Ask the person to slow down or repeat what he or she said. Approach all your conversations as opportunities to connect in a more authentic way, not a chance to judge people or prove yourself right.

Ask yourself:

What evidence are you making up to prove you are right?

What do you gain from proving the other person wrong?

Step Three: Use Empowering Language

"Language is thought," the old saying goes. In my seminars I tell people, "Your language is you." The words you say to yourself create your self-image. The words you say to other people advertise who you are, what you believe, and what you value. The language you use can empower you or keep you trapped in a fear-based perspective.

There is never, never, never, never, never a good reason to disempower yourself or another human being by using unkind language. There is always a way to say what needs to be said in an empowering way. This alone will change how you are seen, heard, and understood. It will alter your image of yourself like no other tool.

For the next hour, Glen and I went over the Four Steps to Innocent Communication you are learning right now. I suggested he call Jessica and apologize for seeing only his point of view. Seeking forgiveness is one way to heal the gap that is left when fear has ravaged our souls. By apologizing, Glen would be taking responsibility for his part in their argument and giving both of them a break. Next, I asked him to confess his love for her and his desire for a future together, whether or not she moved to D.C. This was his way of letting her know that he didn't hold any grudges against her career or her move. He would be showing her that he saw her as innocent. Last, Glen would ask if she would be willing to talk once more about their future together.

Then I coached Glen on the *way* to say it: empowering, compassionate, open, flexible, and inquiring. No more disempowering, condemning, defending, righteous, and accusing. Any time he felt justified in getting angry again, I told him to say, "I'm not sure I understand what you mean. Could you put it differently?" This would give him another opportunity to make sure he heard her correctly. Along with that, he was to focus on understanding Jessica's point of view. Hard as it was, he had to try not to let his fear of losing her distract him from what she was saying.

I asked Glen to study the list of words below. The first column has words that spring from, as well as provoke, fear or mistrust. These are words of expectation, and they make other people (or fate) responsible for your happiness, satisfaction, and love. The second column lists words that are empowering. These are words of intention. They put the power back in your hands by making you accountable for your actions and perceptions.

Expectation	Intention
I should	I decide
I can't	I can
I have to	I choose to
Someday	Today
It's not my fault	I am responsible
I deserve	I commit

I told Glen that while he was talking to Jessica, his job was to attempt to stay with the "intention" words as much as possible. They act as guard rails, keeping your half of the conversation responsible, loving, and non-accusatory. I also shared with him a simple trick that helps me think about the language I choose, particularly when I'm having an intense conversation. Before I say anything, I take a deep breath and look the other person in the eyes. Those few seconds give me time to focus on the words I want to use rather than allowing the words to choose me.

Was Glen going to be perfect in his approach when he phoned

Jessica? Probably not. But with his willingness to see her as innocent, he was more likely to feel connected to himself and Jessica no matter what the outcome.

Ask yourself:

What words of expectation do you use that advertise your fears?

How would you communicate differently if you knew the other person was reacting out of fear?

Step Four: Listen Supportively

To truly listen, you must enter a conversation with no agenda or expectations. You must take each comment at face value. I call this type of listening *supportive listening*. *Supportive* doesn't mean you have to agree with everything the other person says. It does mean you're willing to be receptive, alert, and in the moment.

Supportive listening involves your body language, facial movements, and silence. When you listen supportively, you stay quiet and refrain from interrupting. You make eye contact. You are not daydreaming or recalling another conversation you had last week. With open arms, relaxed posture, and neutral facial features, you signal that you are receptive and nonjudgmental.

The most important part of supportive listening is to stay present. Do not formulate a response while the other person is still talking. If you're planning your next comment during their monologue, you are not present. If you're focused exclusively on proving your point, you won't hear all they have to say. Listening is an opportunity for you to learn something new and maybe even change your own opinion.

Keep an open mind throughout the conversation, and don't assume you know what the other person is going to say. If you tend to categorize people—left wing or right, spiritual or unenlightened, trendy or nerdy—you might also conclude that you know where they stand on every topic. But people aren't that one-dimensional. Give them a chance, and they will probably surprise you. Put your agenda aside and listen for the nuances, the exceptions, the individual voice. Allow people to change, including yourself.

Finally, stay detached. Take the focus off yourself and listen to what is actually being said. Everything isn't about you. Most people want to share *their* experiences, *their* point of view, *their* fears or hopes. When you take things personally, it shows. The other person soon realizes that it's not safe to speak freely because you might get offended or upset.

Supportive listening builds intimacy and trust. It expands vulnerability. It provides new avenues to discover yourself as well as someone else. Supportive listening stretches your limits, broadens your horizons, and moves you beyond the right or wrong of a conversation. It will enable you to see the person in front of you with new eyes.

How a Real Man Handled the Truth

When Glen finally called Jessica, she was understandably upset. She was about to hang up the phone when Glen simply said, "Please. Please don't hang up. I love you." The truth cut through all the barriers to her heart and she was willing to listen.

Glen began by explaining the overpowering feelings that had transpired while they were driving home. He shared how he had secretly made her responsible for them and how he was scared to lose her. His fear convinced him that she loved her career more than their relationship. The situation had seemed black and white to him. And underneath it all, he didn't want to let her know how he was feeling about her because he was afraid of getting hurt. He was afraid she would hold it over him. He was afraid of being used.

In his willingness to see himself as innocent, Glen gave himself permission to be vulnerable. Sure, it was a risk, but you must be willing to risk if you want to love. Fear stops risks from taking place. Love thrives on them.

Jessica listened to what Glen had to say, and then the line was silent for a long while. Finally she spoke up.

"Glen, this job is the opportunity of a lifetime. If I don't take it, I'll always wonder, *What if?* I couldn't live with that. I want to go for it. I want to break the glass ceiling, and this job will do it."

"What did you want to do about us?" Glen cautiously asked.

"I put it out of my mind. You never talked about our future together, so I figured I wasn't that important to you. I can't stay in a 'maybe' relationship. And the truth is, I want this job. It's everything I've worked for."

"I understand. I was afraid to tell you how I felt because I wasn't sure how you felt. I love you, Jessica. And I'm scared to ask, but I gotta. Do you love me?"

"Yes, Glen. I do. I love you."

"Then let's figure out how to make this work."

"You mean it?" she whispered.

"I mean it. How about if we agree to see each other at least twice a month? For the first three months, I'll fly to you since you'll be busy with your new job. After that, we can figure out where to go from there. How does that sound?"

"That sounds great. Thank you, Glen. Thank you for hanging in with me."

How does their story end? To be honest, I don't know. The last

I heard from Glen, they were still seeing each other and the time they spent apart was injecting a good dose of romance into their get-togethers. I do know that when Jessica left later that week, Glen drove her to the airport. And they have long, long conversations over the phone. "They aren't always entirely 'innocent,' " Glen told me with a grin. "But they're always fun."

Earlier in this chapter I said that in order to change your relationships you don't have to believe people are innocent, you just have to act as if they are. That's true, but be prepared: once you give innocence a chance, you *will* believe. It may never be completely automatic, but the ability to see people as innocent is a source of tremendous power. Grab it and use it. Give people the benefit of the doubt. Smile first. Assume they are on your side. Make innocence your default position instead of fear, and watch what happens to your world.

Truth 3

Feelings Lie

I was twenty-four years old when my boyfriend, Jim, seemed to be slipping away from me. I had recently moved to Los Angeles, and he was one of the first people I met. With no friends to speak of, I hung on to Jim more for security than love, but I didn't know it at the time. I was convinced that if he would make me feel loved I would find happiness.

Wanting to appear more confident than I was, I told him I didn't mind if he stayed good friends with his ex-girlfriend. Then one evening, longing for more attention, I began to question him about his ex. Things quickly escalated, and soon I was yelling at him. "You're with me now. And I don't care what I said about it before, you cannot talk to her. If you do, it just proves you are lying to me about loving me. No one who loves me would treat me this way."

In disbelief, he turned to me and quietly said, "I don't know why you're so angry, but it has nothing to do with me." And he walked out the door.

Stunned and ashamed, I secretly knew he was right and loathed myself even more. It felt like another slap in the face in a long line of disappointments. I couldn't stand the thought of living with myself another minute. I grabbed the nearest bottle of pills and systematically took one after the other until the entire contents were in my stomach. I was glad I was going to die. I hated feeling so much longing, sadness, shame, and frustration. It was an unbearable mix of emotions I had to cut off any way I could. I believed I was at the mercy of my feelings. They seemed overpowering as they pushed me around, blamed me for everything, and proved to me that I could not be loved. It was better not to feel at all than to feel as much as I did.

But it was not to be. In the heat of the argument, Jim had forgotten his car keys and instead of escaping he was now forced to face me. Waving the empty pill bottle in his face, I mumbled something about how he would regret it and was secretly pleased that he could see what he had done to me. I was just about to gloat some more when he lifted me over his shoulder and carried me out to his car. I fought him, kicking and screaming, wanting to once again show him how much misery he had caused me. In minutes we approached the emergency room of the local hospital. *Perhaps he does love me after all,* I thought. *Maybe he wants me to live because he can't bear the thought of being without me*. Then Jim unceremoniously dumped me on the curb and drove away, leaving me to the nurses.

What I had feared was true. He didn't love me. And if he didn't love me, who would? I had moved to Los Angeles to hide from myself, and now it appeared my plan hadn't worked. Afraid of being alone, I had attempted to strip myself of any part of me I found unacceptable. I meant to become the perfect girlfriend so that someone would love me. Instead, I ended up being a shell of who I really was, and pretending the drama I acted out with Jim was passion. My fears were running the show.

Love Is More than a Feeling

At the time of my suicide attempt with Jim, I was completely controlled by my feelings. I couldn't identify them, I couldn't process them, I couldn't distinguish between drama and passion, desire and loneliness, love and fear. It was all just a throbbing mess, so it must be love!

One thing is certain: I wasn't alone. In our culture, love is *supposed* to make a mess of us. It comes with a built-in excuse for acting out every passing feeling, no matter how far-fetched or fear-based it may be. We can't help it, the theory goes, because when we're in love we "go out of our heads"—and without a head, all we've got is feelings. We expect to be swept away and to lose control. In fact, we welcome all the confusion. We interpret being out of control as the litmus test of true love, the sign that we've got the real thing.

There is nothing in this world that equals the rush of falling in love, that's for sure. Yet when our desire for love is driven by fear, our feelings of worthlessness or being unlovable can warp our perception of what love is. And without anything to balance our feelings out—such as commitment, intellect, and self-love—they can dominate our senses and override our best interests. Feelings can convince us to stay when we should leave and to settle for less than we deserve. They can even convince us to reject love if it doesn't feel exactly the way we imagine a true love should.

That's how it is for most of us. We let our feelings rule our relationships because we believe they are the most reliable barometer of romance. When things feel good, we stay committed, put in a lot of effort, and are generous and loving. When things feel bad we withdraw, shrug off our promises, become hostile, or cheat. Or we focus all our energy on getting back the supercharged buzz of feelings we had at the beginning of the relationship, never staying in the present long enough to see it for what it is today. Sometimes we stay in a relationship that doesn't really work because it is better to feel something, anything, than to feel nothing at all. When we let feelings run our relationships, they often do a terrible job.

Do you believe love is a feeling? It is, of course. But it is so much more than that. Love is equal parts emotion, commitment, actions, and intellect. It is attitude, energy, and a path. It is at the core of every spiritual philosophy. It expands our heart and is the reason we connect. Love is who we are.

We have a choice.

When we love fearlessly, we can experience our feelings in all their depth and passion without letting them control us. We can recognize that feelings are not facts, they are reactions to the world. We can understand that there is more to love than feeling either blissed-out or desperate, that it is a state of being we create and nourish. When love is based in freedom, we are its partner, not its slave. Our commitments do not waver depending on whether or not it feels good that day. Inspired by freedom, our feelings can guide us to make wise choices about love, even though we have been taught that we have no choice, love just *is*. Feelings have the power to awaken, heal, and transform a relationship if only we channel the insights they provide. The challenge is to honor our feelings yet act on our commitments.

I don't for one moment pretend this is easy. It may be one of the hardest things you ever do. After all, you can't just switch off your feelings. To honor them, you have to become more aware of them, not less. So how do you know which feelings to trust when they are so often based in fear? How do you quit indulging every feeling when they are so overpowering? The first step is to identify what you are feeling. Sound easy? Not for everyone.

"I Am Fine"

Identifying my feelings was my personal Achilles' heel. Being a Midwestern Finnish gal, I was taught that feelings do not matter. You should rise above your feelings, not wallow in them. Specifically, I was discouraged from talking about my feelings. If you don't learn any words to describe your feelings, you have no way to understand them. It doesn't mean you don't feel. It means that as soon as you're out from under the thumb of adult supervision, you tend to act out your feelings as I did with Jim, all the while not having a clue what you are doing or why.

Because I was forbidden to express how I felt about anything or anyone when I was young, I learned three little words that would keep me in good graces with the adults: "I am fine." As an added bonus, "I am fine" also let me avoid reflecting on my own life. "I am fine" was the appropriate answer for any question because, let's face it, no one really wants to know how you feel. They're just asking to be polite, or so I was told.

How are you doing, Rhonda? *I am fine.*

Heard your father killed your mother. *Oh yes, but I am fine.*

Sounds like your life isn't going anywhere. *I'm fine about it.*

When I became friends with Marta, she didn't like my everyday answer, "I am fine." Instead, she would bug me, quiz me, and was downright determined to figure out how I was feeling. I hated it. What was the big deal about feelings? Besides, I didn't know which words corresponded with how I felt. I couldn't pinpoint the differences between anger and frustration. Everything kind of blurred together. It seemed too difficult. But Marta persisted.

At first, feelings were either black or white. I was happy or depressed. Then, with Marta's coaching, I added the word *sad*. What a revelation! When I began to see the subtleties between depression and sadness, a light went on. I could imagine how Helen Keller felt when she finally connected the sensation of water with the word her teacher was spelling in her hand. I'm not seriously comparing myself to Helen Keller, but in my own way I felt as if I had lived in the dark regarding my feelings. And when Marta refused to accept "I am fine," she became my Annie Sullivan.

To help myself, I put together a list of various feelings and kept track of how I was feeling hour after hour. I began to see a pattern. I could see who or what ignited feelings of sadness, frustration, or anger within me, and who or what provoked feelings of happiness, satisfaction, and peace. I could see how I acted on some emotions and didn't act on others. I noticed how my perception of people and events changed when I became aware of the different feelings they sparked in me. And I saw how it worked in reverse, too: if my perception about someone changed based on new information, my feelings would follow. I came to the startling conclusion that no one could *make* me feel anything. Once I was able to identify my feelings, they could literally show me what I thought and what triggered me onto my Wheel of Fear. This was revolutionary and sometimes harrowing. Ken, a man I went out with in my mid-twenties, was the catalyst for my transformation.

We had been dating for a few months when I began to doubt that Ken liked me. I was convinced he was going out with me just to have someone to call his girlfriend. My feelings of worthlessness were overwhelming, and my brain began to dissect every conversation we had and every move he made. Heading for a tailspin, I realized that this amount of emotion was disproportionate to the situation. It was time to do an inventory of my feelings.

It was tough to name them at first, but I finally settled on *angry, hurt, rejected,* and *used*. Good. That was a beginning. Next, I asked myself the crucial question: Am I making this up? Are these feelings based in reality? Do I have evidence to prove Ken is using me? He called regularly and showed up on time. He was always polite, invited me to meet his friends, and surprised me with flowers. If I could just prove I was right, that he was out to use me, I could relax and once again trust my feelings. But there was no evidence to support my fears. The only evidence I had was that I didn't *feel* loved. Then I asked myself the next question: What would make me feel loved? My answer revealed the truth. Nothing. Nothing would make me feel loved. Ken was in an uphill battle against my Wheel of Fear.

I yearned to be loved but I was unwilling to accept the love Ken gave me. It didn't feel the way I expected. His love didn't make all my pain go away. His love was not making me feel beautiful or secure. My fears had me convinced that his love should be different, better, and more.

With my list of feelings in front of me, I was forced to see that the anger, rejection, and hurt I felt were not being generated by Ken. I was rarely around him when those feelings came up. Much as I hated to admit it, the feelings arose only when I began thinking of my past relationships. I was lumping all men together, assuming that if one man (my father) thought I was worthless, all men would. I was just waiting for Ken to prove me right. If I had been able to put aside my fears, I could have clearly seen whether or not Ken and I were a good match. But I wasn't able to, and before long, we drifted apart.

☀ Fearbuster Exercise: ☀ Identify Your Feelings

Identifying your feelings is a critical step in dismantling your Wheel of Fear and approaching other people from a loving and fearless place. For the next twenty-four hours, I'd like you to identify a separate feeling for every hour (or more often if you prefer). Don't get out the dictionary; this is an opportunity to define feelings for yourself, and your definition is all that matters. Be as specific as you can, and when you're done, tally up the five most frequently felt emotions.

If you need help getting started, think of a situation in your past. Now shut your eyes and imagine the situation happening right now. How do you feel? Identifying how you felt in a past situation gives you a safe way to practice. Don't get distracted dwelling in the past, however—you're just tuning up for your twenty-four-hour experiment in feeling identification.

Here's a list of feelings to help you along. Feel free to add your own.

affectionate	defeated	greedy	intimidated
ambivalent	depressed	guilty	jaded
angry	desperate	happy	jealous
anxious	determined	hateful	joyful
ashamed	discouraged	hopeful	judged
beautiful	disturbed	hopeless	lonely
betrayed	embarrassed	humble	loved
bitter	empathetic	humiliated	lustful
brave	empty	hurt	mean
calm	envious	hysterical	melancholy
capable	excited	ignored	misunderstood
cheated	exposed	inadequate	needed
childish	flustered	incompetent	needy
comfortable	foolish	inferior	nervous
competitive	frantic	insecure	obsessed
confident	frustrated	insignificant	oppressed
content	glad	inspired	optimistic
criticized	grateful	irritated	ostracized

overwhelmed	sad	tempted	uptight
passionate	satisfied	tense	victorious
powerful	selfish	threatened	vindictive
powerless	sexy	trapped	vulnerable
pressured	solemn	ugly	wanted
relaxed	stupid	uncertain	worried
relieved	suspicious	understood	worthless
resentful	swamped	unloved	worthy
restless	sympathetic	upset	

Notice that the words *afraid, fearful, frightened, scared,* and *terrified* are not on the list. If possible, I want you to challenge yourself to go beyond these general descriptions of fear. They are usually covering up a core negative feeling you are truly afraid to face. If those words come up for you, fill in the blanks:

I'm afraid (fearful, frightened) that _____. If that happens, _____.

Repeat the phrase until you get to the feeling underneath your fears.

For example: "I'm afraid that I will be rejected. If I'm rejected, people will know I'm inadequate." The feeling you are hiding from is *inadequacy*. Or: "I'm frightened of letting go. If I let go, everything is hopeless." The feeling you don't want to admit you feel is *hopelessness*.

If you find yourself choosing the same words over and over again, I invite you to dig deeper and find the most accurate feeling to describe that state of mind. Do the same exercise, repeating it until you come up with a different, more specific word. For example, if *uncertain* keeps coming up, you might write, "I feel uncertain. When that happens, people will know I'm weak." This will help you identify how you clump feelings together, mislabel them, or disregard feelings altogether.

The Thin Line Between Love and Fear

When you can honestly identify your feelings, a new level of power will open up to you. You will move through confusion more quickly and find it easier to stay on your true path. Nowhere is this more crucial than in relationships, where fear-based feelings often camouflage issues we don't want to confront.

Robin's case was a good example. Sixteen years of marriage and three children hadn't slowed her down—she ran two miles every day and could still fit into her college track shorts. Robin prided herself on knowing the names of all her children's friends and teachers, as well as most of their classmates. She could rattle off the titles of each one's favorite bands, books, and video games. Most surfaces of her home were thickly layered with CDs, school notebooks, and sports paraphernalia. Robin would never win the *Good Housekeeping* award and didn't want to. Her passion for her family outweighed all other concerns.

Yet at forty-two, Robin had reached a turning point in her life. Her children were all in middle or high school, and they didn't need her like they once had. It hurt, but she knew that breaking away from Mom was a natural part of growing up. She wasn't going to be one of those women who insisted on being her teenagers' buddy instead of their mother. She would let them go gracefully. Besides, now she could devote some time to herself. In college she had majored in physical therapy, but she had never gotten the chance to do anything with it. Finally she could resume her career.

It made sense in theory, but in real life Robin's new freedom brought up a lot of fear, specifically that she was not good (smart and experienced) enough to be a physical therapist. There had been tremendous advances in her field, and she would have to go back to school for a graduate degree. Each time one of these frightening thoughts occurred to her, Robin buried it. Itching with pent-up energy and anxiety, she spent hours online researching various graduate programs but couldn't decide on one. Then Neil called.

He had coached her youngest son's softball team for a year, and Robin knew little about him except that he was divorced. Now he was phoning to ask her opinion about purchasing some new equipment. As they chatted about the geekiness of twelve-year-old boys and compared notes on which ones were getting interested in girls, Robin felt her heart racing. How was it that she had never noticed Neil's great sense of humor? And he shared her competitive streak, unlike her husband, Ben, who always called her "manic" for screaming so loudly at the games. On the spur of the moment, Robin offered to meet Neil for coffee and give him her list of equipment sources. Over cappuccino, they talked for an hour and guiltily set up a second date. That evening back at home, Robin tingled with excitement. She took a long bath and thought about the way Neil drank his coffee and laughed at her jokes. It had been years since Ben laughed that hard. The last time she got a haircut, Ben hadn't even noticed. He didn't look at her the way Neil did, with a gleam in his eye. A nice, nasty gleam.

By the time I met with Robin, she was on the verge of having an affair with Neil. "I know I shouldn't do this," she said. "But the feeling is so powerful. I keep asking myself, why shouldn't I feel this way again? Why shouldn't I get swept away? Is it so wrong to want to be loved?" Robin stuck her chin out like a defiant fourteen-year-old. "I know having an affair is risky, but I think it's worth it."

"Why don't you take a *real* risk?" I challenged her. "I don't think you want to sleep with Neil because you're falling in love with him. I think you want to sleep with Neil to distract yourself from your fears." I suspected that Robin was afraid she wouldn't succeed at school or wouldn't like physical therapy anymore once she tried it. She was scared that if that happened, she wouldn't know what to do or who to be. Facing those fears and taking those risks was worth it. Whereas, in my opinion, having an affair was not. "You're pouring all your energy into this man because it feels safer than facing your fears about the future," I shared.

As Robin and I worked through her Wheels of Fear and Freedom, we discovered that she was afraid of being seen as "weak" and that her core negative feeling was "damaged goods." Neil's attention made her feel desirable, daring, and strong. Her relationship with her husband, meanwhile, had withered during the long years of child-raising. Neil saw her as new and vibrant, whereas she was sure Ben saw her as a used-up soccer mom. The physical therapy dilemma had pushed all her fears and insecurities to the forefront. Her passion for Neil felt genuine, but its roots lay within her, not him. Attributing it to Neil was the same as saying she was powerless to experience excitement without him, and that was a lie.

I saw in Robin the same confusion I have seen in other clients: she couldn't differentiate between passion for a person and excitement about life in general. Many times, that is the driving force behind affairs between colleagues, volunteers in political campaigns, cast members in a play, or people who "fall in love" while working together in any type of highly charged arena. All that generalized excitement gets projected onto the nearest warm body, and it feels like love.

Robin felt all charged up because her life was in turmoil. When she met with Neil she felt giddy and shaky, just like a person in the throes of new love would feel. Robin had always assumed passion had to be ignited by an outside force—her husband, her children, and now Neil. She didn't realize that it resided within her, and it was up to her to focus it. Equally important, she needed to know that passion isn't mutually exclusive. We don't have to pick one thing or person to be passionate about and reject all others. If she dared to push herself on to the next phase of her life, she might find that once she regained her footing, her passion for her husband would come flooding back, along with the passion she felt for her new career.

Robin and Ben Go Excavating

When Robin confessed her attraction to Neil, I urged her to come to a few coaching sessions with her husband, Ben, before she took the infatuation any further. No permanent damage had been done, just two coffee dates and a lot of fantasizing. I knew it would take enormous effort for Robin to switch her attention from Neil to her husband, and I wondered how Ben was feeling about his distracted, anxious wife.

As soon as they walked into my office, I could tell Robin wasn't the only unhappy one. Ben, a stocky man in his mid-forties, wore a business suit and a weary expression. His hair was closely cropped, his brown eyes clear and intelligent. He was a good-looking man, obviously health-conscious like his wife. Ben sat at one end of the couch and draped his arms across its back. Robin sat at the other end, clutching her hands. When I began to probe them about their relationship they quickly rose to the occasion and began complaining about the injustices of their marriage.

"The kids are pretty self-sufficient now," Ben said. "Robin finally has some time on her hands, and she deserves it. But is she happy? No. She either mopes around the house or stays glued to the computer. When I come home she barely looks at me long enough to say hello."

"Thank you, Ben," Robin replied. "Thanks for that helpful critique. By the way, the boys aren't out of the house yet. They still need to eat, and I don't notice you cooking. And as far as my moping goes, I'm going back to school and have a lot on my mind. Why can't you be supportive?"

"I'll be supportive when you actually go to school instead of talking about it," Ben replied dismissively.

I let them vent for forty minutes, each insisting that the other wasn't doing his or her part. Finally I interrupted to ask how they felt about each other. They sighed and said nothing for a few moments. Then Ben spoke. "I still love Robin, but it doesn't really feel like we're in love anymore." I wasn't surprised to see Robin tear up and nod her head in agreement.

"I have a homework assignment for you," I said, handing them the feelings list. "For the following week, I'd like you to identify your feelings once an hour, from the time you get up in the morning until you get in bed that night."

"I don't have time to do that," objected Ben.

"You don't have time not to." I assured him. "And in reality, it takes no time at all. Just keep a slip of paper in your pocket, and once an hour stop, choose one word that describes how you feel at that moment, and jot it down."

When we met the next week, I asked Robin and Ben to share their five most frequent feelings. Robin listed *frustrated, lonely, hopeful, envious,* and *needy*. Ben's were *uncertain, satisfied, resentful, embarrassed,* and *vulnerable*. When Robin heard Ben's words she was visibly moved.

"I'm envious that he felt satisfied at all this week. I'm not surprised he felt resentful, because that's how he usually comes across to me. But I'm wondering when he felt vulnerable."

"Every time we were in the same room," Ben said quietly. For the first time in my presence, he looked his wife straight in the eyes. "I wanted to reach out but felt so vulnerable that I didn't have the courage to do it. I'm always afraid you'll yell at me or accuse me of something, and I resent that. I resent how hard it is to talk to you about anything other than the boys. It's as if I don't matter to you at all, just the boys and your search for the perfect graduate program.

"I'm embarrassed by how many feelings I had this week," he continued. "I had no idea how many of the things I do, like working late or going online, are motivated by a need to push away my feelings. And I didn't realize how much I pushed Robin away because I was afraid to be vulnerable."

With that honest admission, Robin and Ben had their best talk in years. During our session, they went through each feeling word they had chosen and gave examples of when it came up for them. Then, with my encouragement, they chose some ways to share their feelings without the added pressure of having to fix everything right away. I have found that although people say they want help solving their problems, in fact they usually open their mouth for one reason and one reason alone: to be heard. Rarely do we find someone who truly listens without either judging us or jumping in to claim that they feel exactly the same way. If a wife says she feels belittled, her husband's response will inevitably be, "Well, *I* feel belittled by *you*!" The greatest gift Robin and Ben could give each other was the space to express their feelings without interruption, so that they both felt heard. When people feel heard, they feel accepted, and that is what most of us are looking for.

It became clear that Robin's "needy" feeling was her Wheel of Fear, disguised as reason, giving her permission to blame Ben for her anxiety and lack of contentment. Ben didn't laugh at her jokes hard enough or notice her haircut—"proof" that he was deficient.

If he were fulfilling her needs she wouldn't be so needy! Her Wheel of Fear told her it was only reasonable that she blame him.

Meanwhile, Ben's "vulnerable" feeling made him afraid he wasn't attractive to Robin any longer and therefore couldn't satisfy her needs. To Ben, vulnerable meant weak, diminished, not sexy. The only place he was able to feel satisfied was at work, so he came home later, which kept Robin's Wheel of Fear spinning. She was sure it was a sign he was losing interest in her, which was partly why Neil seemed so appealing. On my advice, she did not mention Neil to Ben. After all, he wasn't a major player in this marriage, only a small diversion who (thankfully) had stayed that way.

Robin and Ben's assignment for the following week was to sit down each night for thirty minutes and share their top three feelings during that day. No defending or ignoring. No hiding or pretending. I asked them to follow the Four Steps to Innocent Communication that we learned about in the last chapter, and I instructed them to pay special attention to Step Four: Supportive Listening.

A week later they arrived at my office looking hopeful and more relaxed. Things were progressing nicely. Ben explained, "We did what you said. The first night we went back and forth until we shared all three feelings, and we ended up talking for an hour about things that happened in the past that brought up those same feelings. I can't believe how much we haven't been listening to each other, and how often I misinterpreted Robin's feelings. In some situations, the feelings that had cropped up for her were the exact opposite of the ones that cropped up for me! It was eye-opening, to say the least."

Using the Innocent Communication Steps, Robin and Ben were able to move past finger-pointing and start to understand each other better. It was the beginning of a new relationship for both of them.

Like Ben and Robin, most of us claim to have very logical reasons for our behavior: "I must work late to support my family," "I don't have time for my husband because of all my responsibilities." We know that if we add feelings into the mix the situation will start to feel dangerous. We might have to hurt someone or hear something painful, and we want to avoid that at all costs. Yet feelings are usually our only link to the truth of what is really going on between us and the one we love. To love fearlessly, we must be willing to name and share our feelings.

The Secret to Using Your Feelings: Detachment

"All right, Rhonda," you might be saying. "So what if I can identify my feelings? I can talk about them till the cows come home. It doesn't mean I'll be able to do anything about them. You can't control your feelings." Not so fast. Remember, feelings are a result of the information we have and the way we perceive it. When Ben learned that Robin's feelings about some of their past experiences were the polar opposite of his, it changed the way he felt about her in the present. New levels of understanding lead to different feelings, so ultimately we do have power over our feelings. The way to access this power is through detachment.

On the surface of it, you might think detachment is the exact opposite of feelings. One is hot, one is cold. You feel things or you don't. What I mean by detachment is an ability to care and invest, yet at the same time be willing to give up your expectations. Detachment is a crucial step in loving fearlessly. It allows you to let go and love, right now, as is. Not when it gets better or changes, but today. Detaching from the results teaches you how to love deeply without defining the form it takes. When you practice detachment, you allow feelings to come up and honor them as part of your process, yet you are aware that each feeling is not necessarily true beyond that moment.

You already know how to do this. Let's say you don't feel like working. The sun is shining, it's springtime, and you feel trapped and frustrated. Do you quit your job? Probably not. You can detach yourself from your feelings long enough to weigh the consequences of your actions. You realize that feelings change. You know that most of the time you enjoy your job. You understand that to act on your feelings would not be in your best interest. Note that the words *realize*, *know*, and *understand* all have to do with thoughts, not feelings. We use our minds to process our feelings and then decide how to act. The "Identify Your Feelings" Fearbuster Exercise you completed earlier is one way to practice detachment. When you name a feeling, you have more power over whether to act on it or let it move through you, because in the process of identifying it you have separated yourself a little bit from the feeling.

You can learn to treat your feelings about relationships with the same sensibility you use on your other feelings—it's just more difficult because the stakes are higher. When you're in love, it's hard to remove yourself from the surge of emotion, step back, and detach. This isn't news, of course. Most people know when they're too besotted to make smart decisions. However, recognizing it only counts if you do something about it.

After I had been coaching for about six months, I realized that when people asked for guidance about relationships they were usually seeking my detachment as much as my advice or encouragement. Caught up in their feelings, clients wanted me to weigh the pros and cons of their love life objectively. "Think clearly, because I can't," they said. That's fine for people who meet with me once a week, but what about everyone else? And my clients needed to learn for themselves how to detach if they wanted to love fearlessly without my help, which was the ultimate goal. So I created the Love Log.

☀ Fearbuster Exercise: ☀ The Love Log

To tell which feelings you can trust and follow, you must be able to detach from the moment and view the feeling from your truth, your essential nature, the part of you that knows. You can do this by keeping a Love Log. It is essential after a date (more on that in Truth 5), but it is equally powerful with long-term relationships, friendships, and any other connection that is important to you.

Loving always brings consequences. Sometimes the consequences are wonderful, sometimes they are devastating. Most of us focus on love's consequences, but that is not where we learn. It is the process of loving, more than its consequences, that teaches us how to choose a new path or expand the one we are already on. The Love Log tracks your insights about your ability to love. It is one way to understand your process. It helps you to consciously add to your Love Legacy.

If you are in a relationship, I suggest that you make regular entries in your Love Log, especially after a significant event. If you are seeking new friendships, ask yourself the questions after each encounter. And if you are ready to see your place of employment as an opportunity to practice being a loving presence, answer these questions right before you shut down your computer for the night. When you do this daily, it opens your eyes, builds your confidence, and shows you how loving is a choice. In Truth 5, I'll share a special dating version of the Love Log that will help you find your mate.

The Love Log

During this encounter . . .

- What did I learn about my ability to give love?

- What did I learn about my ability to receive love?

- Was I able to see both of us as innocent, regardless of our actions?

- If I could do it over, what would I do differently?

- If I could do it over, what would I do the same?

- How did I feel about myself when I was with this person?

Questions such as, "How did I feel about myself when I was with this person?" tend to result in very straightforward answers. If you felt small, wrong, or insignificant, you will know it. If you felt positive, light, and engaging, you will know that, too. I didn't ask how you felt about the other person because how you feel about *yourself* in these encounters is where the truth lies. Your feelings about the other person may flutter and fluctuate and confuse you: "He's awfully smart, but sometimes he's arrogant, but he's so cute, but he's knows he's cute and that bothers me . . ." and so on into the wee hours. The way you feel about yourself when you are with the other person is a much better measure of the strength, or potential strength, of the relationship. If you consistently walk away from someone feeling more fear than before, it is probably not a good sign. If you are free to express more of yourself, the relationship is a positive force in your life. Complete the Love Log on a regular basis, and your feelings will guide you in the right direction.

Honest Feelings

What if you think you know how you feel, and you are absolutely certain it is based in freedom? Even if the feeling is quite powerful, you could be way off base. Fear-based feelings can derail a new relationship before it has a fighting chance, as it did for the young man who sent me this e-mail:

Dear Rhonda,

Just recently I met someone I was very attracted to. We dated and she told me she wanted to take things slowly. I thought that was fine, and the date was spectacular. Of course, a week later I couldn't wait to tell her I was crazy about her, and I did. That about ended what never really got going. My question is this. Do I just want someone to show me love/affection because I lack some inventory of self-esteem, or am I just a guy who likes to express himself and be honest with the people he likes?

Stephen

Based on the limited information I had, my response was, "Feelings have dictated your actions. You don't know her well enough to be crazy about her. She requested boundaries and you couldn't hold back." Caught up in the moment, Stephen believed he *had* to express his feelings. Yet when he wrote about caring for this woman so soon, it didn't ring true. It seemed as if love were being projected *onto* her rather than occurring *because* of her, and she probably wondered about that herself. Stephen's feelings may have been "honest" at that moment, but three months later he could have felt much differently. I didn't know exactly why he had blurted out his feelings so prematurely, but I'd be surprised if fear didn't play a part in it. My guess is that he wanted to minimize the pain of her possible rejection by testing the waters right away as opposed to waiting. By jumping in so soon to avoid triggering his Wheel of Fear, he got exactly what he was afraid of.

Feelings on Overdrive

One of the great myths about men and women is that men are the cool, rational ones and women are intuitive and feeling-obsessed. Whenever I hear that, I think of Larry. He could be a poster boy for all the men who are accused of being commitment-phobic. Larry wanted to be with a woman who made him feel super special. That's understandable. He also wanted that first-love feeling to last forever. When he met Diane, he spent many months pondering whether he felt absolutely, positively certain that she was The One. He had to feel ready to commit. It had to feel right. But then Diane found out she was pregnant. A month before the baby was due they got married. But five years and a second baby daughter later, Larry still had one foot out the door. He just wasn't sure how he felt about Diane.

A high school science teacher, Larry was accustomed to critiquing his students, grading tests, and passing judgment. Diane was his temperamental opposite, a graphic artist who spent much of the day alone in her studio. When Larry arrived home in the early afternoon, the baby was napping and five-year-old Amanda was still at after-school care. It could have been a time for the couple to reconnect. Instead, Larry found himself brooding and reexamining his feelings about his wife. Was he as attracted to Diane as he had been when they first met? Did he find her as funny? As kind? Was Diane irritating him or pleasing him that day? Was she paying attention to him or devoting all her energy to the baby? Larry interpreted his shifting emotions about Diane as proof of an unsteady relationship. Unless the marriage felt great ninety-eight percent of the time, he feared it wasn't working the way it should.

I gave Larry the Love Log and told him to answer the questions every night for a week, then come back and see me. When he did, he admitted that it had been an extremely difficult assignment. "I found out some rather unpleasant stuff," he said. "What did I learn about my ability to give love? That I don't try to give it very often, I'm sorry to say. Was I willing to see both of us as innocent? Not at all. I only viewed myself as innocent."

Larry told me that his biggest complaint since baby Kelly was born was that Diane wasn't as nice to him as she used to be. "I liked her old, mellow, relaxed self. I liked us the way we were before. Having Kelly has definitely added more changes to her life. I know she's tired now—I'm tired, too—but it's not fair of her to take it out on me. I've been angry about that, and I definitely viewed her as the villain. Anyway, I started treating Diane as innocent, only because you told me to. I forced myself to stop blaming her. By the end of the week we were getting along better than we have in months. She doesn't even know why—I didn't tell her I was doing this. I'm too embarrassed by what I'm finding out about myself."

"How do you feel about yourself when you're with Diane?"

"I know she loves me. I feel safe, comfortable. Loved."

"Then you have a choice. You can release yourself from your

obsessive re-evaluation of your relationship. You, not Diane, are the one creating that reality and giving time and energy to those feelings. You could be spending it loving instead of judging. The next time you feel yourself shift into judging mode, stop. Identify the feeling. Remember your essential nature, and act from that higher place."

"I know you're right," Larry said. "But I'm not sure I can change."

"You can," I assured him. "You just have to think about your relationship a little differently. Are you committed to your marriage, or to your wife?"

"I don't get what you mean. It's the same thing."

"Not at all. Change what you're committed to, and everything else will fall into place."

The Golden Door: Commitment

Feelings are powerful but fickle. They can send us into the stratosphere, or land us on the curb outside the hospital. They can teach us, but they can't lead us. What can? Commitment.

Living fearlessly and with intention puts commitment at the forefront of your life. What are you committed to? Are you committed to a person, or to a job, or to something larger? Are you committed to a way of life? An attitude? A way of being?

You must be committed if you want to love fearlessly. Committed to staying true to yourself. Committed to accepting yourself as is. Committed to standing up for what you believe in. Committed to expressing your essential nature so that on each date, or with your mate, all of you comes shining through. And once you have found that person and made the choice to love, you must stay committed to the relationship. Not the person, not the feeling, the relationship.

When I asked Larry whether he was committed to his marriage or his wife, he responded the same way all my clients do: "What's the difference?" The difference is that in a relationship, you are not committing to the other person but to the two of you together. The sum is larger than the parts. When you are committed to the relationship, you aim for a different standard than your day-to-day feelings about your mate. If your intention is to be loving, you don't think, "I'm out of here," every time he or she does something that irritates you. Your emotional temperature doesn't rise and fall in response to the other person's.

Larry's attention had been focused on his reactions to Diane instead of the bigger picture, their family. "Refocus," I told him. "Remember that you're committed to something larger than Diane, with her ups and downs and ordinary human frailties. You're committed to the essence of why you two—and now, you four—are together. The funny thing is, if you are committed to the relationship, it's easier to stop taking things so personally. You can witness Diane's mood swings, and your own, without worrying that it's all going to fall apart. If you are committed to your marriage, you don't need to keep re-deciding about Diane. Let her moods roll off you, and be loving. You won't succeed every time—you're not Gandhi—but you can change your feelings if you identify them and remember your commitment."

Being committed doesn't mean you can't end a relationship if it becomes unsalvageable or abusive. You can and should end any relationship that might harm you or your children. Commitment is not a blind vow, it is an act of faith made with your eyes wide open. Loving fearlessly, you make a commitment like this only with someone who sees and loves you for who you are, someone whom you desire to know better than any other being on the planet, whom you want to practice accepting and loving unconditionally. As long as your commitment with this person stands, there is no room for questioning, doubling back, or maneuvering. There is only one answer, and that is, "Let's work it out."

I encountered what was, for me, a big test of commitment a month before my wedding to Carl, to whom I was married for seven years. We were sitting on the couch cuddling and I smelled cigarettes. He didn't smoke, although I knew he had in the past. "Have you been smoking?" I teased, thinking he had probably just been around someone else who was.

"Well, yes," he admitted. Feelings welled up inside me—betrayal, anger, confusion, and helplessness. I wanted to run out the door screaming, "Noooooooo! This is the man I'm going to marry. This is the man I love. He can't smoke. This isn't happening!" My feelings may seem disproportionate to you, perhaps, but that is exactly how I felt. I loathed smoking, and refused to date anyone who had a pack of cigarettes in his pocket. "This must be some cosmic joke," I remember thinking. But I was committed to our future together, so this time I stopped myself from coming undone. Instead, I sat there in silence and carefully thought about how to handle it, somehow sensing that a lot was riding on my reaction. Finally I told Carl the truth, as simply and lovingly as I could.

"You know, honey, that really scares me. I want to spend the rest of my life with you and I'm afraid you're telling me you don't want to live."

To my surprise, Carl admitted that he too was scared. Scared of getting married. Scared of not being able to provide for me. Scared of not making me happy. Scared of disappointing me. I kept quiet during his confession, giving him an opportunity to feel his own feelings. By the end of our talk, we had both cried, hugged, and learned to trust each other a little bit more. Through the years he continued to struggle with the habit, which came and went depending on how he felt about himself. But I never confused his struggle with tobacco with his commitment to our marriage.

I don't know about you, but everything I have ever done that I am proud of started with a commitment. Whenever I have gotten into the muck and mire of my journey, there has always been a place of choice, and my commitment gave me clarity. If you don't know what you are committed to, just look at your choices. They continually reinforce your commitments whether you like it or not. They define what you deem important. With most couples, the place of choice is the altar. It doesn't matter if, until now, you have kept one foot out the door. You can make the choice to become fearlessly committed to your relationship today, and start focusing on it instead of your feelings or your mate.

I understand there will be days when you don't want to go ahead, when you are tired of doing the right thing, when you feel like life is a series of tasks that have nothing to do with you. When that happens, sit down and remember that *you* chose this life, you wanted this commitment. Feelings are the energy that drives us, the charge that makes the hard work worthwhile, the juice in the apple. Yet in love, many times your biggest challenge will be to honor your feelings, express them, process them, yet take actions based on your commitment. Commitments fuel your staying power. Your relationship may last twenty years, it may last one, but while you're there, be committed. I won't pretend it isn't hard sometimes. Commitments always test us beyond what we think we are capable of. That is their purpose—to keep us focused on what matters most, so that feelings don't choose for us.

Commitments stretch us. They push us past our comfort zone.

They invite us to have more faith and find love in unexpected places. They dare us to surrender to something grander than we ever imagined, something beyond a passing feeling or infatuation, beyond fear and insecurities. Commitments lead us to the place where we can stop, look around, and say, "I'm home."

Truth 4

Chemistry Is Between
Your Ears

I'll never forget the first time I saw Chris. I was chatting with some friends on the way into church, and when I turned around, there he was. I stopped in mid-sentence. From under shaggy bangs a pair of startling green eyes gazed into mine. I briefly registered the rest of him—faded jeans, T-shirt, and sneakers. He was not my type. Not at all. Except for those eyes.

Just before we went to our seats, Chris whispered, "How can I get in touch with you?" I frantically searched my handbag for a business card, to no avail. All I had was my workshop flyer for the following night. As I handed it to him, someone grabbed me and started talking about that day's guest speaker. When I turned around, Chris was gone.

Now I would have to wait. Would he call? Did he feel the same thing I felt? Would he come to my workshop? The next thirty-six hours were painfully slow. I rationalized falling in love and rationalized staying out. I lectured myself on the myth of love at first sight. I built evidence about how his sneakers were a sure sign we weren't meant to be together. I checked my horoscope.

But on Monday night I was ready, just in case. I wore my long black skirt with slits up the side, casual but sexy. I made sure my sweater accentuated my best features. Then it dawned on me that if he did come to the workshop, he might become either a client or my boyfriend. What if eradicating fear was on his agenda instead of falling in love? What if he saw me only as a teacher? I pushed the thought out of my mind. I had to stay focused or I knew my fears would take control. I decided I would follow his lead.

At five after seven, Chris walked in, sneakers and all. My heart started pounding like a teenager's. After the workshop, he hung around until everyone else had left. I kept myself busy for a few minutes straightening chairs and cleaning up, trying to figure out some way to give him a "yes" so that he would feel comfortable enough to ask me out. Finally I resorted to a tried-and-true girl tactic and announced, "I sure am hungry."

"You are? Right now?" he asked instantly. "Me too. I'd love to take you to dinner." And we were off. At a nearby diner we talked for hours, captivated by every tidbit of information we could learn about each other. We ordered cup after cup of tea, unable to leave. When at last we floated out of there, we made plans to have our first official date on Friday night. Chris told me he wanted to show me his new house and asked me to arrive around seven.

You can imagine the hours I spent getting ready—clothes, hair, scented oils, the works. Heck, this could be my next husband. I knew I'd remember this night forever, but nothing could have prepared me for what was waiting inside Chris's house. A hundred candles were lit, setting off his place in a dreamy, fairy-tale glow. A Sarah McLachlan album played softly in the background. It was romantic beyond words. This is what I had been missing in my marriage, I thought to myself. Between kisses, we ended up sharing the same story about how we both *knew* we were meant for each other. When it started to get late, we couldn't bear to separate, so we half-talked, half-kissed, and half fell asleep in each other's arms. One of the aspects of loving fearlessly is placing lust behind commitment, and in alignment with that I promised myself I wouldn't get intimately involved with Chris until there was a commitment between us. I kept that promise, but it was torture.

When we woke up on his couch around five in the morning, I mentioned something about having to go home and he started kissing me again. We ended up spending all day Saturday together, and I broke away only long enough to go back home, take a shower, grab some fresh clothes, and meet Chris for the evening.

By Sunday he looked at me and simply said, "Will you be my girlfriend?"

"Yes," I replied, feeling that all was right with the world. We were both convinced this was *it*. On Monday morning I was telling everyone I had found the man I was going to marry. While I was phoning my friends with the good news, Chris was confessing the same thing to his business partner. It was instant, all-consuming, heart-stopping chemistry for both of us.

It was good for a month. We stayed together for three. The first was dazzling, but by the second and third I was tormented. I was still wildly attracted to Chris, but I had been practicing Fearless Living for a few years and could see that we weren't a good match except for the amazing passion we shared. I knew I had to end it, but I was afraid if I saw him in person I would lose my willpower. I was that smitten.

Finally I wrote him a letter:

"The love I felt for you still exists, yet what has kept us together for the past three months cannot sustain a lifelong commitment. This relationship has taught me that I can feel passion and keep my senses about me at the same time. And I am grateful. Good-bye, Chris."

He called me a few days later. "I've never been dumped with so much grace," he said ruefully. We got together the following week, and he admitted he hadn't been emotionally prepared for the depth of our relationship. I confessed that I had ignored all my own dating advice with him. I felt we had been so busy being "in love" that we never took the time to build a foundation that would make love last. It was all too fast, too soon, and too much. We never really got to know each other.

Chris gave me a wonderful gift when we talked about our relationship so honestly. Because of our open-hearted communication, my fears faded a little bit that day and my Love Legacy was changed for the better. Our breakup was not filled with accusations or excuses, and Chris and I were able to remain friends. I still see him in church occasionally, and every now and then I'll get a fleeting memory of those spine-tingling first few weeks. The thought will leap to mind, "What was *that* all about?" But I know the answer. It was chemistry.

Most of us have figured out by the age of twenty-five that sexual chemistry alone doesn't guarantee commitment or happiness. But it's so hard to resist! The crowd disappears, the room spins, and all we can see is the object of our desire. It feels all-consuming, a force much greater than mere willpower. *This time it will be different*, we think. *This person will love me, understand me, and make me whole*. We want to believe the spark we feel is a sign telling us, "This is The One." It isn't wrong to want a clear signal, but chemistry is not it. Chemistry is only one ingredient of long-lasting love—perhaps the least reliable one.

Sexual chemistry can rock your world when you experience it full-force and haunt you when you don't. For most people, the fears that surround chemistry are more powerful than chemistry itself—fear of never having it, having it but losing it, having it with the wrong person, or falling under its spell and losing everything else because of it. I have found that the myth of sexual chemistry influences people's decisions about love much more than they would ever admit to themselves. The expectation of intense passion can keep people single for years, searching for the perfect lover who will always light their fire and never get boring. I have listened to both men and women say, "What's love without chemistry? If you don't feel that thrill, why bother?" I have witnessed perfectly well-matched couples make the fatal mistake of thinking that fading chemistry is fading love.

Yet I have also seen men and women who were friends for years suddenly decide to marry, and those marriages have worked. I have met couples who have been together five, ten, or twenty years and are obviously happy, and I don't think they're lighting a hundred candles for each other every night. True love—the deep, committed, fearless kind—happens with sexual chemistry, without it, and sometimes only after the first, intense heat has burned off.

Even if you are vigilant about watching where your feelings are coming from, the pull of chemistry can sweep you off your feet. I got swept away by Chris, and I'll confess I have been tempted since. Each time, however, the Fearless Loving Truths explained in this book saved me from mistaking a magnificent affair with a true love. They have taught me that to love fearlessly, you must embrace chemistry for the powerful gifts it brings, while staying aware of its limitations.

Chemistry Explained

Obviously, the lust you feel for a stranger across a crowded room has nothing to do with his or her personality. If pressed to explain it, most people would say it's something in the way she moves, smiles, or laughs. It's something in the way he lifts a package or pushes back his hair. But beyond those vague cues, what draws us to one type over another? That question has intrigued philosophers and scientists for thousands of years. Over the past century psychologists have added their voices to the chorus. Some theorize that instant attraction depends on your early experience of love—your Love Legacy. We are captivated by people who possess the traits our parents had, and we register those traits unconsciously. For instance, if the woman across the room sips from her drink the same way your mom did, you get turned on. That woman makes you feel warm and safe, although you probably aren't conscious of the reason.

On the scientific front, some researchers believe we are attracted to people whose physical features would result in the most successful offspring, which would explain why women are drawn to big, husky guys and men are attracted to women with good child-bearing qualities, such as wide hips. (But *are* we drawn to those types today? Most of the current screen goddesses are built like twelve-year-old boys with a pair of balloons attached to their chests.) In the lab, all sorts of exotic studies have been conducted to determine whether sexual chemistry is closely tied to pheromones, scents we emit that alter the behavior of other people. In one study, men and women were told to sniff sweaty T-shirts and rate them according to sexual appeal. In another, men were tested to see if they could detect fertility in women by their smell and if they found fertile women more attractive than those who were not. Although some of the studies concluded that men and women do notice differences caused by pheromones, there is very little consensus about how they react to those differences.

From a Fearless perspective, we are attracted to people whose fears are either similar to our own or somehow complement them. It is as if our Wheel of Fear is seeking our mate for us. When you first meet someone, your Wheel picks up on cues that indicate a match—a comment, a roll of the eyes, a joke that signals, "I'm on your wavelength." You recognize a kindred spirit and it gets your blood racing. If my fear trigger thought is, "I am a loser," it makes sense that I would want to hook up with someone who is afraid of being rejected. That way, he probably won't leave me. And what about two losers together? Think of the powerful bond you have with someone when you share the same excuses about why your life has stalled out. It takes only a few minutes to establish this connection, and then the chemistry starts to bubble.

Which of these theories is correct? Maybe they all contain elements of truth. The only clear-cut piece of the chemistry puzzle is the biological reaction that takes place when you meet someone who, for whatever reasons, strikes the right sexual chord. All at once, your body is flooded with phenylethylamine (PEA), an adrenaline-like neurochemical. Dopamine and norepinephrine, which are similar to amphetamines, also come into play, making your heart beat faster and your mood soar. Together, PEA, dopamine, and norepinephrine are the "chemistry" that sets your body tingling and puts your fantasies into overdrive.

In Truth 2, I mentioned that six months is a nationwide silent contract and that many relationships falter at that time. Six months also happens to be the point at which the first blaze of sexual chemistry usually begins to fade. No matter how strong the initial attraction, it is almost inevitable that chemistry will wear off sometime between six months and three years. This may be why the social landscape is littered with people who can't sustain a relationship longer than a year or so. "The chemistry is gone," they will complain, and off they'll go, looking for someone new to give them that chemical rush. But the search for permanent chemistry is doomed. What's more, there is evidence that our bodies build up a tolerance to the high of sexual chemistry. As we move from relationship to relationship, it takes more intense doses to satisfy us.

The good news for couples who make a long-term commitment is that, in time, a new group of chemicals will replace the hypercharged chemistry of early love. These are endorphins, which provide an opiate-like sense of peace and security. Long-term couples also enjoy the effects of the chemical oxytocin, which has been called the cuddling chemical. Either emotional or physical cues can prompt the production of oxytocin, which makes people feel calm, supportive, and loving. This long-term chemistry is available to every couple, not just those who were electrified by sexual chemistry at first glance.

As a relationship moves from the fireworks of first love to a deeper, more complicated romance, the chemistry will change. At that point, the attitude you bring to your beloved will have a profound impact on the chemistry you feel. Intimacy, vulnerability, and trust will start to matter more as you actually get to know the target of your desire. Eventually, the fantasy you projected onto the sexy stranger will have to be reconciled with the man or woman standing before you. You will have to open your eyes and connect, person to person. You will have to think and choose. You will have to talk and listen. That is why they say that the human body's most erogenous zone is between the ears. Chemistry is real, but the ingredients are in your head.

Emily's Story: Where Did the Spark Go?

Emily was twenty-eight and had the sort of clear, pale skin and soft curly hair that reminded me of an English country lass. As she stood looking around my office, I watched to see where she would sit—in one of the deep velvet chairs, or on the more severe sofa? She chose the velvet, of course. Emily oozed sensuality. That's why she had come to see me.

"I'm in a relationship, but I don't think he's the right man for me. There's no chemistry," she announced.

"How long have you been seeing him?"

"It's been almost two years. We've been living together for a little over six months. At first I thought he was my perfect match, at least physically. But it isn't the same anymore."

"So you did have chemistry with him at one time?"

"Oh, yes, in the beginning we did. He was a hot young guy, five years younger than me. My girlfriends all said I was robbing the cradle."

"When did the chemistry stop?"

"About four months ago it just got up and left. I've tried to get it back, but it just isn't there. I want some help getting out of this relationship without hurting him, and then I want you to show me how to date so this doesn't happen again."

Emily and Jeff had met at the self-serve car wash. They had hosed down their vehicles in adjoining stalls, eyeing each other and flirting all the while. To Emily's surprise, the obviously younger Jeff had asked for her phone number before she drove off. Because she was the older one, Emily felt as if she were in control of the relationship, and the power of it had made the sex even better. She did things she wouldn't have dreamed of doing with anyone else, told Jeff her most outrageous sexual fantasies, and expressed herself freely in every way, no holds barred. In the dark, she also shared her dreams and plans for the future. Before Emily realized it, she had opened up and told Jeff just about everything. Then they moved in together. It had been hot and heavy up until four months ago.

"Why did you decide to live together? Did you want to marry him?"

"I never thought that far ahead, and we didn't discuss it."

"Has Jeff ever mentioned it?"

"Hmmm. I'm not sure. Oh wait, yes he did. I remember that one day out of the blue Jeff casually mentioned that he didn't want to get married until he was thirty. So that was the end of that. If he and I got married, I'd be thirty-five! It seems ancient."

"When did that happen?"

"I don't know. A few months ago."

"Right about when the chemistry stopped?"

"It was about the same time, you're right. I sure am glad I've cooled down about him sexually. Otherwise, breaking up would be a lot harder than it already is."

It was time to give Emily another perspective. "I think when Jeff told you he wasn't interested in getting married, you became scared of being rejected. You became disinterested in order to protect yourself. Think about it. If you leave, there's nothing wrong with you, right? You're just being mature, leaving a younger man to look for a more realistic relationship. That is, unless you love Jeff."

"I never said I loved him."

She didn't have me convinced. When couples begin their relationship in a burst of sexual passion, the real thing—love—can come as a sobering shock. As a fling, Jeff posed no threat to Emily. She could toss aside her inhibitions and tell herself she was evolved because she could enjoy sex without love. Sex usually makes us feel vulnerable, but when the chemistry is so intense, just the opposite happens—we feel invulnerable. Passion overrides everything else. Emily felt like Superwoman, but even though she had told Jeff so much about herself, they had never talked seriously about their future or their feelings for each other. They didn't share a solid foundation of emotional intimacy.

When she and Jeff moved in together, the dynamics changed. Jeff became a potential mate, whether or not Emily allowed herself to think about it. His comment about marriage finally tipped the cart. Rather than a titillation, his age was now an obstacle to future happiness. Jeff may have made the comment to see if Emily cared for him, or perhaps he was tired of living with her and was trying to send her a message. There was also the possibility that it was nothing more than an offhand remark. The point, however, wasn't to guess what Jeff meant. The point was that his comment had triggered Emily's fears, and now she had to make some decisions.

"Chemistry is what brought you two together," I said. "But chemistry alone can't sustain a relationship. If you feel that Jeff could be the one for you, you'll have to tell him you're getting serious. And I suggest you ask him whether he was serious about waiting until he's thirty to marry."

It was time for Emily to speak the truth. Did she love Jeff or not? Was she tired of him or afraid of being rejected? Was she willing to leave if he didn't want a commitment? Was she willing to get married if he did? She had to answer these questions if she wanted to be fearless. In the end, Emily knew she would feel like a fake if she didn't face her fear of being rejected. She chose to talk to Jeff, although it didn't come out as she had planned.

"I told him I'd been feeling very distant lately," Emily recounted. "He said he had noticed and had wondered what was wrong. But instead of acting loving, I blurted out that he was too young for me and I needed to break it off. He confronted me head on and asked if this was really about his age. I tried to shrug it off. I was really uncomfortable, but he persisted so I told him the truth. I told him about marriage, his age policy, and how it made me feel."

"Then what happened?" I was on the edge of my seat.

"He laughed. Can you believe it? I didn't know what to do. The next thing I knew, he was down on his knees proposing to me. I practically fainted."

"What was your answer?"

"You already know, Rhonda—it was yes."

"And the chemistry?"

"Oh, that's fine again. I realized from our sessions that when I start feeling insecure or under stress, I shut down sexually. Now I know that about myself, and I won't blame Jeff for my lack of passion."

Slow-Burning Chemistry

Emily and Jeff hit the jackpot: instant chemistry that evolved into real love. It doesn't happen that way for everyone (including me). In fact, their situation is the exception. But many people do experience red-hot chemistry at some point in their lives, and it definitely leaves its mark. They may end the affair, but the memory stays with them. And once they have tasted mind-bending passion, they can't imagine settling for anything less. On the other end of the spectrum are people who tell me they are willing to forego chemistry in order to have a solid relationship. These men and women come into my office with a no-nonsense, I'm-gonna-take-control attitude that's fine for job hunting but a little off-base for romance. I'm teaching Fearless Loving here, not Fearless Deal-Making. People who hold out for instant heat are missing the boat, but so are those who cross chemistry off their list altogether.

Natalie, age fifty-one, was sent to me by her good friend Lisa, a long-time client of mine. She had a dry sense of humor and enough material about the dating scene to support a stand-up act. "Sure, the movies say we can have it all. You know who gets to have it all? Meg Ryan. And even *she* can't have it all in real life! Chemistry is for teenagers. Having someone fix your computer or clean up after you is about as romantic as you're going to get in a husband." But despite her jokes, Natalie was serious about finding someone to love, so I began to guide her through my dating program (which you will learn about in Truth 5). Shortly after we began our sessions, she met Paul through mutual friends. He was nice enough. Kind enough. Worked hard enough. They had things in common.

"But there is absolutely no chemistry," she sighed.

"I thought you didn't care about chemistry," I reminded her.

"I don't. I swear I don't. But when I'm sitting there, thinking about the rest of my life . . ." Natalie shook her head as if she were disgusted with herself. "I know it's a pipe dream, but I want to feel excited about someone again, and I just don't feel it with Paul."

If you have never been in a committed relationship and shared true, lifelong, can-count-on-it chemistry, the only kind you're going to recognize is the instant lust you've either experienced or heard rumors about. On every date, you're hoping to be struck by lightning. Unfortunately, if you're like most of us, the first few dates are almost guaranteed to stifle chemistry, even between people who might be a great match. Why? Because on the typical first date, your focus is on impressing the other person. All your defenses are up. You are on your best behavior, dressed to kill, and watching every word you say. There is no way you are going to reveal your essential nature, not until you know you're safe. You are also spending a lot of energy sizing up your date's looks, style, manners, and opinions. Of course, what you're seeing has little to do with that person's essential nature, since your date is also on his or her best behavior. The two of you are circling, judging, holding back, sucking in your stomachs, impressing, worrying. Chemistry *may* begin to smolder under those circumstances, but it's more likely that you are both too distracted to see the other person's essence, and ultimately that essence is what will ignite true love's chemistry.

In our session after her first date with Paul, Natalie and I went through her Love Legacy to uncover how sexual chemistry had affected her previous relationships. The woman who had declared, "Chemistry is for teenagers" admitted that three affairs in her past had been fueled by lust. In each one, Natalie had called chemistry "love" and made it her excuse to stay with a man who wasn't right for her. She had wanted excitement, and if she didn't feel immediate chemistry with someone, she dropped him after the first date.

Natalie's fear trigger was being thought of as "ordinary." Her sense of self-worth was tied into a desire to be brighter, funnier, and more dangerous than the average woman. She had always fallen for bad boys who could give her a good fight when she needed to feel alive—the drama kept the chemistry percolating. Better yet, all the shouting, fighting, and making up kept Natalie from dwelling on her deepest fear: that she was just an ordinary woman who wasn't good enough to be loved by a "high-quality" man.

As we sat together and talked about how her fears had led to heartaches in the past, Natalie told me that her fiftieth birthday had been a turning point for her. She had decided to forget about chemistry and just concentrate on meeting a decent man. "Paul fits the bill," I told her. "You said you didn't care about chemistry. Maybe it turns out that you do. Either way, why not put aside your assumptions about chemistry for a while and see what happens with Paul?"

As part of my dating plan, I insist that clients date the same person three times. There are a few exceptions: If your date is rude, mistreats you in any way, or is a substance abuser, your first date is your last date. But Paul was a nice guy, so per our agreement she went on a second date with him. Her conclusion was the same, no chemistry. She begged me to get out of date three, but my answer was simply, "No."

On the third date, something curious happened.

"I was relieved it was our last date," she explained. "Paul was nice but there was no excitement. So instead of worrying about what he was thinking about me every two seconds, I just sat back and listened. When I did that, something changed. I was no longer trying to impress him or figure him out, I just experienced him for who he was. And I hate to admit it, but I started to like him. I liked the way he talked to me. His kindness was evident on date one but it didn't really appeal to me until date three. He was so nice to everyone we met. I knew then that it wasn't an act but a genuine part of who he was. I realized that sitting before me was a real, live, high-quality human being, maybe the first I had ever dated."

As date three turned into date thirty, wedding bells began to ring. Even more exciting was that after the third date, chemistry magically appeared. It wasn't the electric jolt of lust triggered by a stranger whose fears meshed with hers, but a slow, sweet, deeper chemistry that grew from a true connection of the heart. Today, Natalie and Paul are happily married. If instant chemistry had been the guidepost, their relationship wouldn't have stood a chance.

A Few Words about the Unmentionable

Sexuality is one of the most powerful of all human drives. We both crave and fear intense sexual chemistry because we have been taught that when it strikes, we're going to fall into our lover's arms and never be able to climb out. In fact, we are considered fools if we *don't* follow our desires. Sex is on our minds not only because we are human but also because the society we live in uses it to sell everything from dishes to tires. It's hard to open a magazine, turn on the television, or walk down a street without seeing dozens of images of gorgeous, sexy men and women. And music doesn't help. Song after song is about lips, eyes, burning desire, yearning for a lover's touch, you name it. If we confuse sexual chemistry with love, it may be because so many different voices have told us that it *is* love. It is up to us to notice what is happening and take responsibility for our own sexuality.

When we are not sexually satisfied, thoughts of sex can seep into nearly every area of our lives. As time goes by and we haven't connected with someone, people we ordinarily wouldn't consider sharing a taxi with start to seem passable. This is dangerous territory, especially for women. Men have an advantage over us—when they feel aroused and there is no partner in sight, most men don't hesitate to take care of things themselves. Even in this enlightened age, many women are uneasy reading the word *masturbation*, much less doing it. Satisfying yourself is a powerful defense against the lure of sex with strangers, yet quite of few of my female clients have told me they are too ashamed, guilt-ridden, or uncomfortable with their own bodies to take the plunge. Before I send you into the wide world of dating, I'd like to share what I have learned about masturbation and chemistry.

First, a confession. I used to be one of those women who refused to touch herself, even if I really, really needed to. My reason? Pride. *I have a man to do that for me,* I told myself. *Only losers resort to masturbation.* (Remember, "loser" is my Wheel of Fear trigger thought.) Then I coached a woman from an extremely religious background, where masturbation was expressly forbidden. A boyfriend had introduced her to the concept when she was in her late twenties, and as she explained how the knowledge had altered her attitude toward dating, I couldn't help but see parallels to my own situation.

"My life would have been completely different if someone had taught me how to do it when I was sixteen," Carolee told me. "I wouldn't have relied on men so much, gone from man to man. The only way I could fulfill myself physically was through a man. It didn't even occur to me that I could give myself an orgasm. I wouldn't have comprehended why someone would want to. I experienced my first sexual turn-on when I had intercourse, and I assumed it was the only way to be satisfied. Then Russell showed me a magazine article about how a woman could touch herself during sex and have a better time. I was amazed and embarrassed, but excited, too. I have to give him credit for letting me see that my sexuality didn't belong to him, it belonged to me."

There was no way to avoid comparisons between my own attitude and Carolee's before her enlightenment. I too went from man to man, looking for someone with whom I had chemistry. I didn't grasp that it was natural to feel aroused. I always assumed it was just chemistry between me and the man of the moment. It was as if my sexuality were entirely in the hands of the men I dated, and I was just a passenger.

During the seven years I was married to Carl, sex wasn't high on my priority list, but after my divorce I found myself back in the dating scene again with a desire to experience sex differently. This time around, I vowed that I would give myself pleasure whenever I needed to and not feel like a loser for doing it. And I found out it has added side benefits. Lou Paget, sex educator and author of *How to be a Great Lover,* says, "How do you ask for what you want if you aren't even sure what that is? Self-pleasuring gives you that information and makes it available for you to share with your partner." I realized that by taking care of my needs I was not only educating myself but also improving my sex life. Beyond feeling good, there was a higher goal: I wanted to keep a clear head around men. I didn't want chemistry to sway me from my commitment to living and loving fearlessly.

Today, when a client wants my help finding romance, the first thing I discuss is her relationship with her body. Can she look at herself in a mirror without the voice of ridicule going off in her head? Does she allow herself the pleasure of being touched through massage? Is she physical with her body through exercise or outdoor activities? Does she think of lotion as a remedy for dry skin or as a pleasurable treat for her body?

If it becomes clear that a woman is reserving touch for her next sexual encounter, I encourage her to begin exploring herself with something simple, such as putting scented lotion on her body. To get accustomed to being touched by someone else, I advise massages. It is amazing how so many women see these self-caring activities as indulgences. To me, they are necessities. Massages keep me aware of my skin and muscles and grateful for the pleasure they give me. Scented lotion reminds me that I am beautiful and sexual. Dressing in front of the mirror allows me to practice loving myself, cellulite and all. And hiking, biking, skiing, and other physical activities remind me how lucky I am to be housed in a living, breathing body. And the same goes for my male clients.

I always tell my shier clients about Carolee and urge them to explore their own bodies. I advise them to put romance into their lives right now, without waiting for The One.

Lust for Life

Long-lasting chemistry is between your ears, and if you doubt it, consider the results of numerous studies that asked men what they found most sexually appealing in a woman. It was not the size of their breasts, the color of their hair, or the length of their legs. It was their confidence. Men love a woman who is not afraid to be herself, and that usually shows up first in her body language. When you feel comfortable in your skin, it shows in the way you move, sit, laugh, even the way you eat. When you feel sensual at home or walking around your neighborhood or talking with friends—not just with a man—sensuality becomes a part of your essential nature. It draws people to you and allows you to experience passion more deeply when you do connect with the right person.

Just as loving yourself brings more love into your life, loving your body brings more pleasure into your life, with or without a partner. While none of us can ever tame sexual chemistry (and who would want to?), if our sensuality belongs to us, we can see chemistry for what it is, enjoy it when we are fortunate enough to find it, and step back when the chemistry is right but the person is wrong. In the next chapter, I am going to show you exactly how it works in the real-life chemistry lab—dating.

Truth 5

Dating Is Where You Practice Being Yourself

I firmly believe there are amazing people all around us seeking the same thing we are: healthy, loving relationships. And I believe that when we don't have those relationships, it's usually because we are standing in our own way. If you are willing to take a long, hard look at your Love Legacy; to see people as innocent; to think about your feelings before you act on them; and to acknowledge both the power and the limits of chemistry, you are ready to step out fearlessly and find love. I'm talking about dating, but not like you've done it before. As for all of you who are already in a relationship, do not skip these pages. You probably know someone single who could learn a lot here, so pass it along. It might even open your eyes to an unseen aspect of your present relationship, or shed some light on why your past relationships failed while this one stays intact.

The dating philosophy I'm going to share with you in this chapter isn't like other dating schemes you've read about. It is not about finding someone to rescue or fix you. It is not a series of ploys that requires you to hide your essential nature, your intentions, or your character. In fact, it's just the opposite—Fearless

113

Dating requires you to be true to yourself. The truer you are, the better it works on every level. It makes you more confident, loving, joyous, and relaxed. It makes you more fun to be around and more appreciative of the people around you. Believe it or not, you will actually enjoy dating once you learn to do it fearlessly.

Because my coaching is all about overcoming fear, I've been able to pinpoint the aspects of dating that people find most intimidating. Clients tell me they hate small talk and the need to impress someone new. They are tired of putting on an act, of pretending to be smarter, sexier, wealthier, more creative, more athletic, or better connected than they really are. They don't want to lure someone in under false pretenses. They are weary of trying to "hook" a partner; they want real love. And like everyone else, my clients have a core fear that they are not good enough. This belief makes them downplay, hide, or lie about certain aspects of themselves so the other person won't reject them. The cover-up only makes things worse, however, because of an inescapable Catch-22: If you don't let people see who you really are, they cannot love who you really are. In other words, you will never feel truly loved. Your hidden fears will always be there to remind you that they don't know the *real* you.

This is the emotional tension that runs beneath most first (and second and third) dates. We long to connect, but we don't want to reveal ourselves. We crave intimacy, but true intimacy takes time and we don't want to wait. So we look for the easiest, quickest connection: sexual chemistry. We jump in, get swept away, and hope or believe that in the end we'll love the person. It seldom works out that way.

I wanted my clients to be able to approach dating from a whole new perspective. When I thought about the fears that stalled them out in their search for love, I realized that the answers were already in front of me. The principles of Fearless Living, when applied to dating, pointed the way.

Fearless Dating is foolproof because it helps you discover who you are, what you want, and the things you stand for. Instead of dating solely to nab a mate, you are dating to practice being yourself. The ultimate goal of Fearless Dating is to find a lifetime partner, but that is definitely not its only goal. You use dating to connect with others not as potential soul mates but as potential friends. Within that liberating attitude, love has room to grow. You approach each date with a specific intention, not about the other person but about yourself. Along the way, you gain clarity, and your encounters gain new focus. Dating becomes less intense and at the same time more purposeful. Your path to self-knowledge merges with your path to connection.

The clients who have used this approach have had tremendous success, but you must follow each of the six steps. (Your desire to omit a step will tell you which aspect of dating you fear.) Don't skimp on your commitment. Stay completely honest with yourself. Be fearless in your approach, keep a loving attitude, and have faith. Here we go.

Step One: Choose the Top Five Qualities You Seek In a Mate

First I want you to take out a piece of paper and, in fifteen minutes, write down all the qualities you would like in a partner. Your goal is to list fifty of them. Don't stop to think or judge yourself, just write down every quality that pops into your head. If you get to thirty-two and just can't think of another trait, that's all right, but try to get to fifty.

Some people freeze at the thought of actually listing what they want. Others resist this step, thinking they've done it before and it didn't work, so what's the point? I remind them that this list is step one; the rest of the Fearless Dating plan is like nothing they have done before. I've also had clients tell me that writing a list seems too practical; they would prefer love to just appear "naturally" in their lives. That would be nice, but the wait-and-hope method isn't very effective for most people, especially once they are out of school and are no longer exposed to dozens of new faces each semester. The truth is, writing this list will bring your longing for a relationship out of dreamland and into the real world, and that makes some people feel very vulnerable. They're scared of having to find out whether the soul mate they fantasize about actually exists, so they start objecting that the list is too premeditated—"Love should be spontaneous!"

Listing what you want does not mean you and your future partner won't be spontaneous. The list does put the responsibility for what you desire into your hands, and that can feel like pressure. Good. Better you feel pressured to think about what you want now, as opposed to when you're on a date and your fears are up. So start writing! Put down every characteristic you have ever desired, dreamed about, contemplated, or envied, no matter how small. Some traits appear on almost everyone's list, for example, most of us would like a partner who is reasonably attractive, has a good sense of humor, is intelligent, and can support him- or herself. Women often want a man who would like to have a family. Men sometimes want a woman who will be a financial partner and find meaning in her work. Many people won't tolerate smokers. And there will be qualities on your list that will be particular to you. You may fancy a guy who likes to go biking or a woman who is into bluegrass music. Write down character traits such as compassion, curiosity, a romantic nature, and courage, and preferences such as a love of movies or travel. You might want someone who puts kindness first or makes personal growth a priority. Perhaps an adventurous spirit or a playful nature turns you on. If you are on roll after fifteen minutes, keep writing until you reach fifty or can't think of anything else.

Next, I want you to narrow those traits down to twenty. That's right. I want you to name the top twenty characteristics you couldn't possibly live without. Then I want you to pick the top five traits that you absolutely must have in a mate. This may be difficult, so take the time to really think it over. These five traits will be your compass for the rest of the program. Whatever you do, don't cheat and simply write down five traits. The process only has value if you start with as many as you can think of and hone it down to five.

Honesty is absolutely essential in this process, even if you have to admit things about yourself that may not make you proud. Perhaps a taut, toned body is very important to you. You realize some people might think it's superficial, but there it is. You want a 10. So be it! You will, of course, need to ask yourself whether *you* are a 10. If you're not, in the months to come you will discover whether you have other qualities that will attract and hold a spectacular, body-pumping man or woman. Perhaps you will discover that you want to redefine what 10 means to you, or you may decide that a 7 or 8 will do quite nicely after all.

Terri was in her late thirties when she came to see me. She sat tensely on the edge of her chair smoothing the skirt of her linen suit. Terri owned her own business, a travel agency specializing in corporate groups. When I asked how her career was going she told me it was fine and that she enjoyed her work. However, she wasn't meeting the sort of men she could see as lifetime partners or the father of her children. She couldn't quite put her finger on what was wrong, but they all seemed too young.

"Are they actually younger than you?"

"No, I usually date guys who are a few years older."

"Well then, what makes them seem so young?"

"Maybe it's the way they act at restaurants. When the check comes and we go to split it they're always so precise about it. As if every penny counts. That seems immature to me."

We went around with it for about ten minutes, and then I simply asked her, "You want a man with money, don't you?"

"No, I don't!" She was shocked at the suggestion. "I believe men and women should be equals."

"Wanting a man with money does not mean you won't be his equal. Power isn't only about your bankbook. True power is being willing to declare what you want and face the reasons you don't think you deserve it. Again, that's just fear talking. So Terri, if you don't admit it, I can't help you find him."

I knew Terri came from an upper-class background and was accustomed to that world. Her business earned her a good living, but it didn't put her in the rarefied income bracket she was used to. Terri had convinced herself that she should date men with whom she could be on equal footing financially so that they could "share power." The plan was failing because neither her work nor the men were satisfying her. She said she liked her job, but I could tell she wasn't passionate about it. An hour later, she finally confronted the truth.

"I should want to work, especially in a business I created myself. But I don't really care about it. I'm ashamed to admit it, but what excites me is the thought of living in suburbia, doing the mom things. I want a baby more than anything. I feel like such a phony."

"I'm not here to judge you," I told her. "I'm only here to get to the bottom line and help you find what you really want. If you only want a man to supply sperm, Fearless Dating isn't the answer. It is not the solution for our hidden agendas."

"I do want children, but not more than a finding the man who would be my Mr. Wonderful. I want a great husband first, then a great father for my children. And yes, I would like him to have more than enough money in the bank," Terri answered, clearly embarrassed.

"Then let's put it down as one of the top five traits: a man who can support you so you can focus on family."

Now, it may seem as if everyone, men as well as women, would like the luxury of not having to work for a living. In reality, very few people can honestly list "wealthy" among the top five traits they seek in a lifetime mate. It might make the top ten or fifteen, but rarely the top five. For Terri, it was different. She finally admitted to herself that having money, social standing, and the freedom not to work for a living was extremely important to her. She wanted to raise children, not stock options. Terri is now married to a very wealthy man.

It's quite possible that as time goes by and you alter your perceptions of the world, your top five traits will evolve. That's perfectly all right, as long as you're not changing your mind every few weeks (which amounts to not really selecting just five qualities). The challenge is to be scrupulously honest with yourself and stay focused on those five qualities when you date new people. Often my clients will say, "Well, he's got five of the top fifty—numbers three, fifteen, twenty-five, thirty-one, and forty-seven." That will only lead to dating "potential." Fearless Loving is not about dating and mating potential. It is not about hoping someone will transform themselves or blossom before your eyes due to your loving support. Potential is exactly why people stay in relationships way too long. We see numbers three, fifteen, twenty-five, thirty-one, and forty-seven, and pray they will add up to one hundred percent happiness. But they never do. It has to be the top five qualities. No exceptions.

I'm not asking you to do something I haven't done myself, by the way. I know how hard it is to choose those five qualities. I've selected compassion, integrity, a generous spirit, intelligence, and lightheartedness. A couple of times I've come awfully close, but I have not yet found a man who possesses all five. Meanwhile, being aware of my top five qualities has acted like a safety belt, preventing me from "accidentally" (impulsively) getting too involved with men who are wrong for me. Your top five qualities will do the same for you. I'm not saying you won't make a false move now and then, as I have. The point is, since I have discovered this concept I have not invested years in a false move. I have always been able to pull back and keep those five qualities in my sights.

Folks who are already in a serious, committed relationship have also gained a lot of insight from this first step. I urge you to try it and see for yourself. Understanding your top five qualities will help you figure out why you complain about what you do and why your mate sometimes frustrates the heck out of you. Being aware of your top traits will help you refocus on what matters most and will remind you why you fell in love in the first place. It will definitely give you some perspective on your ever-evolving relationship.

Step Two: Define Your Top Five Qualities

This is a crucial step that will help you clarify exactly what it is you are seeking. Human qualities are subjective—your definition of *generous* might be quite different than mine. In this case, the only definition that matters is yours. Do not use a dictionary. Do not ask your friends. Don't let any outside influences affect your personal definitions, or they won't be true for you.

Jordan told me he wanted to meet someone who had a good sense of humor. "What kind of humor?" I queried. "The joke-telling kind? The laugh at anything kind? The laugh at yourself kind? Do you want someone who can laugh along with the boys, or someone who is a great audience for your jokes?"

"Ummm . . . I don't know."

"This is the time to really think about your past relationships. Have you ever dated someone or had a friend with the qualities you seek? Can you describe those qualities? Try listing the type of humor you missed in other girlfriends."

After thinking it over, Jordan came up with the following definition of the humorous woman he was looking for:

- Someone who can laugh at herself while at the same time taking responsibility if she's made a mistake.

- Doesn't use humor to deflect problems but uses it to lighten up a tense situation.

- Sees the world from a humorous angle; doesn't take things too seriously.

- Uses humor to make others feel comfortable.

Nowhere in his definition did Jordan say he wanted a woman who liked stand-up comedy or saw the world as one big joke. While writing his definition, he realized how in the past he had made humor black or white. You either had it or you didn't. Now he was able to see the subtleties.

"It makes so much sense. When I was writing it down I realized that I had been holding myself to an impossible standard of humor. I want a woman I can laugh with, but I thought that meant I always had to be 'on'—cracking jokes and making clever observations twenty-four hours a day. I see now that it isn't about being ha-ha funny. My humor is more subtle, and I began to appreciate it for the first time rather than comparing myself to professional comedians."

Defining your top five traits not only clarifies what you yearn for, it also shines a light on your own qualities. Getting specific becomes a reality check. It's amazing how many people want their mate to have qualities they themselves have not cultivated. There's a bit of magical thinking behind this desire—on some level, they believe that if their partner has a certain quality, they'll automatically get it, too. If he reads a lot, she'll be smarter. If she runs two miles a day, he'll get in shape. It's not a conscious connection, but fantasies about intellectual conversations or shared workouts start popping up when they imagine life with their ideal mate. While it is true that your partner can be a good influence, it is also true that people tend to gravitate toward others who already possess the qualities they value, not to people who would *like* to possess them.

Claire, for example, put "healthy lifestyle" at the top of her list. Yet she was sixty pounds overweight and had done little to change it since we began our work together. Delicately, I pointed out that a man who was healthy might not view her as particularly compatible. If she was serious about wanting a healthy mate, she had to ask herself whether she was healthy.

"Well, last year I gave up bread, and this year I'm going to start walking every day," she said.

"The minute you start walking in earnest you'll attract different

men, and I'm sure they will be more healthy than those you attracted in the past."

Claire didn't have to become a buffed babe, but she did have to
take responsibility for her own health. Five months later, she was
thirty pounds lighter and delighted with her new body image. She
power-walked around the lake near her home four times a week
with a walking club after she dropped her kids off at school. The
last time we spoke, Claire told me that a male member of the club
had asked her out for coffee. I don't know what will develop between them, but I do know that Claire is more ready than she ever
has been to connect with a healthy man. Literally, she is walking
the talk.

Step Three: The Dating Questions

Once you finally select your top five qualities, how do you discover if the person you are dating possesses them? Some traits,
like a sense of humor, are obvious. Others, such as the person's
hobbies or taste in music, are easy to talk about. But many qualities are difficult to uncover, and you don't want to ask nosy questions that will put your date on the hot seat. How, for instance, can
you tell if someone is reliable, ethical, good with kids, or kind to
his or her parents? By telling stories rather than asking questions.

For each quality you're curious about, come up with a few relevant anecdotes either from the newspaper or your own experience. Let's say one of your top qualities, like mine, is compassion.
In that case, you would share a story that had compassion as an
underlying theme, such as one about the closing of a factory, a cus-
tody battle, or some other incident where the conflict had no clear
solution. Don't choose stories where the right response is obvious.

Then, listen carefully to your date's reaction. Is he quick to judge, or does he think about it carefully? Is he tolerant or rigid? Can he admit to not being able to decide how he feels? You might also relate a situation where *you* had difficulty being compassionate. Does he empathize with you or judge you harshly? Is he compassionate toward you and your struggle? Or does he fail to see what the dilemma was in the first place? Stay detached and alert, and make mental notes for your Dating Log (Step Six).

Qualities such as being ethical, respectful, or compassionate also reveal themselves in a person's actions. I've heard it said that you can tell how someone is going to treat you by observing the way he or she treats the waitress. It's not bad advice. Being an ex-waitress myself, I also try to get a glimpse of the tip a man leaves. It's not an absolute guarantee of a generous spirit (one of my top qualities), but it's a pretty good indication.

Step Four: The First Three Dates

When you have settled on the top five traits you want in a partner, the way you view the opposite sex will change radically. Men and women who have gone through this process with me have described how it gave them the clarity they needed to see dating differently. They became detached. They were able to quickly eliminate choices that in the past would have frustrated or confused them. They no longer used their feelings to decide who to spend time with, but instead used their heads. They did not rely on chemistry! They didn't get distracted by someone's vague plans for the future or smooth talk, but calmly observed where the person was at that moment in his or her life.

Step Four has to do with what occurs on the dates themselves.

I have a few guidelines for this, and I'm very serious about them. First, I enforce a dress code: When you go on a date, you must wear the clothes you prefer in everyday life. No dressing to fit into someone else's idea of what's hot. No dressing to impress. If you're a jeans type, you wear jeans. If you feel most comfortable in a business suit, you wear that. Obviously, your clothing has to be appropriate for the locale, but stay true to your own style.

As I shared with you in Truth 4, I insist on a three-date minimum with any person who may possess your top five traits, as long as he or she isn't cruel and doesn't have a behavior you can't tolerate, such as smoking or substance abuse. I don't believe you can get to know someone in fewer than three dates, especially when you're trying to discover if he or she has your top five qualities.

Each of the three dates has a time limit. The first may last no longer than one hour. That means it is probably going to be a casual date such as lunch or coffee. You cannot go out to dinner on the first date. The second date can last two hours, max—maybe enough time for dinner, but not dinner and a movie. On date number three, you are allowed three to four hours. Please be sure to meet in public places for all three dates to stay safe. And on at least one of the three dates, you must change some part of the arrangements—the time, the place you're meeting, or the day (I'll explain why shortly). Call first, of course, and give your date enough time to reschedule as necessary.

This formula is a clear departure from the typical date, where you stay out as long as you're having a good time or as long as the other person can convince you to stay. Rather than being in charge, most of us leave it to fate and chemistry. Three dates with time limits is a much better idea, for a number of reasons.

First of all, time limits keep you from telling too much too soon. If I had kept to a time limit when I first went out with Chris, the green-eyed honey I met at church, I might have avoided falling so hard and then having to pull back so quickly. Instead, we spent all night in the coffee shop sharing our secrets and creating a false sense of intimacy. By the end of that marathon first date, we thought we knew all about each other. We were wrong. When you spread out your introduction over three dates, you protect yourself from the illusion of instant intimacy. In between dates, you have time to think about the person and decide what you would like to find out next time. And if there is chemistry between you, the time limits protect you from letting yourself get too swept away.

All these reasons ought to be enough to help you see the wisdom of this approach. But the main purpose for setting time limits and changing at least one of the dates is to see if the other person will respect your boundaries. To put it bluntly, you are searching for signs that your date is potentially controlling or abusive. I've advised you to see everyone as innocent, but occasionally you might meet someone who is not. Given what happened with my mother and father, I'm very sensitive to domestic abuse, be it mental or physical. The warning signs can be easy to spot if you know what to look for. Pressuring women to do things they don't want to do is a flashing red light. Typically, the pressure begins with something very minor, such as:

"Can I buy you a drink?"

"No thanks, it's too early for me."

"Oh, come on. You can handle it."

"Really, no thanks."

"Listen, I hate to drink alone. Why don't I just order a glass of wine for you, and you don't have to touch it if you don't want to?"

"Well, all right."

Bingo. He's just pegged you as someone he can control. His goal isn't to get you drunk, it's to get you to bend to his will. Certain women (and men) are particularly susceptible to abusers, but no one is entirely immune. Their take-charge attitude can seem sexy and charming; their intense interest in you can feel flattering. But if you could tell from the first date that a charmer was likely to hurt you, wouldn't you run? The time limits on the first three dates are like a trap. Controllers, manipulators, and charmers can't resist pressuring you to stay beyond your limit, thus revealing their true colors. They also dislike change because it brings up their feelings of powerlessness. By changing the time, date, or location on one of your dates, you can test their flexibility and willingness to share control.

Incidentally, you don't have to explain this strategy to the people you go out with. No need to announce, "I'd love to go to your place, but I'm following Rhonda's Fearless Dating!" Just set things up so that you can easily stick to your limits. Meet for lunch on a workday so you'll have a built-in reason to end the date—"Gotta get back to the office." At night, make plans for after your date, such as stopping off at a friend's house. Use your head, and don't let passing feelings or chemistry throw you off track.

Step Five: Choose an Intention

In Truth 4, I told you about Natalie, who only realized she had chemistry with Paul after they had gone out on date number three. She admitted it took her that long to forget about judging him and really listen to what he had to say. In the spirit of nonjudgmental listening as well as general self-improvement, before you go out on each date set a specific intention for yourself. It's a powerful exercise in self-discovery, it gives you another reason to date, it helps you practice being both fearless and loving, and it distracts you from scrutinizing your date's every move.

Your intention will have nothing to do with gathering information about your date's five qualities. Your intention will have everything to do with you. For example, it may be to refrain from speaking ill about any family member. Or you may vow not to fib about any opinion, even if you're afraid your date won't approve. You may choose to speak up or listen extra hard. You may promise yourself to talk about something you love to do. You might decide to practice being more generous, lighthearted, or flexible. Whatever you choose, it ought to put you a little closer to your essential nature. Make it an intention that is valuable to your own growth regardless of how the date goes.

After my divorce, I decided it was time to take my own advice. I set an intention to have a voice. It may seem easy to you, but years of staying silent so I would be loved had taken their toll. Sure, I was able to speak to thousands of people about fear, but talk to a man? Forget it.

I had been dating Jack for about a month when my intention was put to the test. We were at his house and just about to go eat when he casually mentioned that he'd like to check the football scores. Being an ex-football widow, I understood. He grabbed the remote and started flipping channels. I had seen this before. All was going well, and then he sat down. Uh-oh. When a man sat down in front of football, my experience was that he would continue to sit for hours. I was devastated, but I had my intention: Speak up, have a voice.

Whenever I am working on a new intention, I do not leave home without the phone number of a friend I can call if my fear becomes too much to handle alone. After a few minutes, I excused myself and went into the next room with my cell phone. I dialed Marta's number and reported my crisis in a trembling voice. "He's watching sports. He sat down. He won't get up. This is awful."

"Tell him you're ready to do something else," Marta said calmly.

"What? Are you crazy? I can't do that. I mean, I told him that it was okay to check the scores. It's his house, for gosh sakes. I can't tell him what to do in his own house. We were on our way out to eat, but now . . ." My voice trailed off.

"He checked the scores. Tell him you are ready to go and eat."

"Didn't you hear me? I can't do that."

"Do you want to watch sports?"

"No."

"Are you ready to go and eat?"

"Yes." That's when I burst into tears. I knew I had to say something, but the thought of doing it made me a nervous wreck. He would think I was selfish and worthless. He would certainly think I reneged on saying yes to checking the scores. It all seemed black and white to me, even though I knew that wasn't the case. He had checked the scores. We were on our way out. He did ask me out. If he liked me, he would want to please me. Oh, how I hated this.

"Have a voice, speak up, say your truth," Marta encouraged me. Tears were streaming down my face and I had definitely been gone for twenty minutes. Marta's voice interrupted my thoughts. "Rhonda, if you are unable to ask him to turn off the TV, let's figure out another way to get you back to center. Why don't you tell him you're going for a walk and ask him to join you. You can do it, Rhonda."

Right. I could do that. Then he could decide if he wanted to come with me or not, but at least I could get myself out of this hellish situation. I nodded, told Marta exactly what I would say to Jack, hung up the phone, and made my way to the bathroom to survey the damage to my face. My nose was red and my eyes were puffy. This was going to be so embarrassing. What if he asked what was wrong?

After a little powder and lipstick, I walked to the couch, sat down next to him and . . . nothing. I could not get a word out. For ten minutes I sat on that couch with his arm around me pretending to watch the game. *Rhonda, what is your intention?* My focus came back to what this date was really about for me. It wasn't about whether he liked me or not. It wasn't about whether I liked him. It wasn't about finding Mr. Right. It was about speaking up, being true to myself, having a voice. Anything else was icing. Speaking up was the cake. I knew I had to do it.

"Jack, I'm going to take a walk while you finish checking the scores, unless you want to come with me?" Okay, it was a little wimpy but at least I got it out.

"Sure. That sounds great." And with that, he turned off the TV and grabbed his shoes.

My jaw dropped. *Is that all there is to it?* I thought. *Is it that easy?* But I knew it wasn't about that. For the first time in years I had spoken up to a man I liked. And the best part was, it helped heal all the times I hadn't done so in the past. It gave me the courage to do it again.

For a year I practiced making simple requests of the men I was dating: Could we see this movie? Would you walk to the mailbox with me? Would you listen to a problem I am having? Would you make me a cup of tea? I was building up my self-esteem in the area of making requests so when it came time to make the big requests (big for me, that is), I would have a solid foundation to lean on.

Step Six: The Dating Log

As you have probably noticed, Fearless Dating is all about being focused. One very effective way to stay laser-sharp is to keep a record of your impressions of each date in a Dating Log. The Dating Log is similar to the Love Log from Truth 3, except that this has an extra benefit—it helps you find your mate.

As soon as you arrive home from a date, open a notebook (or computer file) and jot down your observations. The act of writing will force you to articulate your feelings and think a bit harder than you otherwise might. In each entry, answer the following questions:

- How did I feel about myself when I was with this person?

- How did I feel about myself after the date?

- What would I do differently on my next date with this person?

- What would I do the same?

- Does this person possess any of my top five traits? If so, which ones?

- What action did I take that was based on my commitment to love fearlessly?

- What was my special intention for this date? How did I do?

As I mentioned in Truth 3, focusing on how you feel about *yourself* after a date is a good way to gauge the relationship's potential. Your feelings for the other person may be swayed by chemistry or a lack of it, or by biases about the person's job, background, or appearance. How you feel about yourself matters the most. If being around the person makes you feel strong, happy, and secure in yourself, it's a sign that at the very least you may have found a new friend.

If during your date you begin to doubt yourself or feel insignificant or bad in any way, take a deep breath. Examine those feelings under the guidance of your Dating Log and see if they come up regardless of who you are with. Continue to go on three dates to learn to differentiate your "I am scared to death" feelings from "This person is scary" feelings. Fearful feelings that stem from your perceptions do not always reflect reality. Facing them will give you a chance to heal. Of course, boundary violators who can't hear 'no' do not get past date one.

The Dating Log is a guidance system that will give you clues about where you get hung up, stuck, or afraid. It also points out your insights and transformations. The tenth time you write, "I felt stupid," you might call it a fear instead of using it to beat yourself up. The third time you write about feeling guilty after a date, you might ask yourself some questions about your motivations for seeing the person.

After my date with Jack—which went very well as soon as we left the house—I grabbed my Dating Log to get some perspective on how I felt.

- How did I feel about myself when I was with Jack?
  When he asked me questions, I felt heard. And when he gave me a compliment about my work, I felt seen. I was proud that I took the risk of going out on a date. I felt strong because when he tried to kiss me good-bye and I felt uncomfortable, I expressed it. He apologized.

- How did I feel about myself after the date?
  I felt empowered and valued. I felt sexy and attractive, two qualities I haven't felt in quite a while. I set a small boundary

regarding the kiss and that made me feel more sure about what I wanted. I'll feel more confident for the next date.

- What would I do differently on my next date with Jack?
  I would not break the silence with conversation. I would allow conversation to stop and start instead of thinking I had to entertain him.

- What would I do the same?
  I was proud of myself that I accepted his compliments without minimizing them. I was proud of the way I asked him a question that in the past I would have thought was stupid. And of course, stopping the kiss.

- Does this person possess any of my top five traits? If so, which ones?
  Yes. He has integrity. He arrived on time, made reservations at the restaurant we agreed upon, and when he accepted a call on his cell phone he was brief. He warned me he would be getting the call and explained his reason without apologizing too much.

- What action did I take that was based on my commitment to love fearlessly?
  I put boundaries in place without feeling guilty for it.

- What was my special intention for this date? How did I do?
  My intention was to speak up. I asked Jack to come for a walk with me so he would turn off the football scores. *Yes!*

That little date was the beginning of my newfound self-confidence regarding my relationships with men. In the past, I would have focused only on what the man might be thinking of me. I would have told all my friends about him and quizzed them for their opinions instead of deciding for myself. The Dating Log empowered me to take part in the dating process like I never had before. My self-esteem increased with each date I went on because I knew what changes I was making and the risks I was taking. Previously, all I would have cared about was how I was feeling about the guy. My own well-being would not have been part of the picture.

This time around, I was not only including myself, I was also learning to trust myself. The Dating Log gave me the tool I needed to empower myself and keep clear on my intention. No more letting him off the hook because of how I felt about him. Feelings were secondary. As I began to trust myself more, I was able to determine more quickly who aligned with my top five qualities and who did not. No more back and forth depending on my mood. When I wrote in that Log, I came away with a strong sense of me.

What About Sex?

One more thing about Fearless Dating. You are not allowed to sleep with the other person on any of your three dates. That's right, no sex. You know why. But in case you're tempted to forget, I'll explain my reasoning.

When you have sex too soon, it's easy to confuse chemistry with love. You feel fantastic, so you think, "Why not make love? What's the big deal? This might be it!" You talk yourself into believing that having spontaneous sex means you are free, fearless, and willing to take a risk. But this is sexual chemistry talking, not love. That's why I advise my clients not to get into bed with anyone until they truly know the person is commitment material. The self-imposed waiting period gives them time to differentiate be-tween feelings that are based on chemistry and those that spring from a deeper attraction.

A real risk would be to put sex aside, even as a topic of conver-sation, until you and your date get to know each other beyond the obvious chemistry. I have noticed that if a man brings up his sex-ual desires on the first date, even if it's couched in humor, he is ad-vertising what matters most to him. Don't disregard sexual jokes and innuendoes. If sex is on his mind to the point where he feels he's got to talk about it, sex may be *all* that is on his mind. And don't assume that the sexual wordplay is proof you two are in sync, not even if the other person says, "You're so easy to talk to." That's one of the oldest lines in the book! Unless you have had some difficult conversations—about commitment, for instance—of course you'll be easy to talk to.

I know that some of you may have used sexual chemistry as a strategy to filter people in or out of your life. Heck, if they are will-ing to dive in, if they can't control themselves, it must mean they want you. Stop. This is a warning. He (or she) wants your body, not necessarily the real you. If the person you are dating isn't will-ing to have a conversation about commitment, or if you aren't, how safe do you really feel? Do you want to spend a lot of time, perhaps years, with someone who is reluctant to talk about what you mean to them and what your relationship represents? I wouldn't, not anymore. In the past, I would have rationalized that we didn't need to talk about commitment because the man was at-tentive, phoned regularly, got my car fixed for me—whatever I could use to convince myself the relationship was solid. "Why be so insecure? Trust him, Rhonda," I would have told myself. That was fear talking. It helped me avoid feeling worthless around a man I might be falling in love with. Yet my unwillingness to insist on a spoken commitment eventually made me feel even more worthless, not to mention insecure.

If you want to be really fearless, I encourage you to hold off on sex until you and your partner have made a commitment—an agreement to be monogamous and to move forward, together, in the same direction with similar intentions. Not implied, not suggested, but talked about, affirmed, and agreed to. You might call it safe sex. Or smart sex. Or fearless sex. It is a challenge, but a worthy one.

Small Talk, Deep Talk: The Myth of Instant Intimacy

No chapter about dating would be complete without mentioning the part that grates on singles the most: small talk. Women, in particular, say, "All his small talk is boring and pointless. He's too shallow, not deep enough for me. I want to know how he *feels* about things. Whether he wants children. What his plans are for the future."

Excuse me, but why should someone you have just met divulge all this personal information? Most people don't feel comfortable doing that until they trust you, and the way to build trust is through small talk, not instant soul-baring.

Small talk is a social skill that is essential and appropriate when you're dating someone new. Through small talk, you can reveal yourself in layers. First you bond over the mundane—food, movies, current events, mutual friends. Slowly, you step into your vulnerable areas and begin exposing yourself. You watch the other person's reaction. If you feel secure, understood, and heard, you keep upping the ante. You share more and more of who you are as trust expands.

The problem is, we want love so badly that we often mistake a deep conversation with intimacy. We share too much of ourselves too quickly, thinking it will make us close. It doesn't work that way. Intimacy is cultivated over time. You can't rush it or create it all at once by confessing your innermost thoughts to someone who is basically a stranger. That person will still be a stranger when you're done confessing—a stranger who knows too much about you. In fact, the next day (or week) you may very well resent your date for knowing so much. You may be embarrassed by what you revealed or afraid of what he or she might do with the information. All those fears may lead you to back off in self-preservation. By leapfrogging over small talk into deep talk, you may short-circuit the potential for true intimacy.

And what about the person who tells you every secret on the first date? Do you really want to know that much? How can you process it when you have no context for it, no knowledge of his or her behavior, values, or history?

This is what happened to Sarah. On their first date, Cameron went through his entire romantic history including his two marriages, three live-in girlfriends, and numerous casual relationships. He thought he was being up-front and open. Sarah, meanwhile, was overwhelmed with this outpouring of vital statistics. She could tell he was trying to be honest, yet they had barely finished their first cup of coffee and this confession was not welcomed or invited. They never got to date two.

The truth is, intimacy starts with the ability to have a casual conversation. Small talk keeps your connection alive. If it's boring or pointless, maybe that's your fault. Long-term couples don't spend most of their time in deep discussion about the Big Issues. They spend it making small talk, joking around, and gabbing about everyday events. It's exhausting to be deep all the time. It's also unnecessary. Small talk is part of everyday life and everyday awareness, and if you think you want deep all the time, you're kidding yourself.

Of course, the reason so many people are impatient with small talk and want to move right into deep talk is that for them, each date is fraught with life-altering significance. Each new person might be The One, and it's urgent to find out if that's the case *right now*. But why put yourself though all that? If you're following Fearless Dating, you will gain from the experience even if your date isn't The One. To take the psychological pressure off, I often suggest that my clients replace the word *date* with *friend*. When you see dating as building friendships, small talk becomes more enjoyable. Finding out about the other person's favorite band or vacation spot doesn't seem trite, it seems informative. The whole experience feels safer and more comfortable when you have no expectations on the line.

Where the Good People Are

The Six Steps I have shared with you can set in motion a spirit of Fearless Loving that will help you claim your essential nature as well as make you a more desirable friend or a lover. It's an inner shift. When you stay true to yourself, overnight soul mates and instant chemistry become less important. Instead of the irresistible sexy stranger, you'll seek out people who have the top five traits you desire. And you will find that, just like you, most of them are longing to connect.

If you are one of those people who insist that all the good men and women are taken, I have a challenge for you. I don't think you are serious about dating. Have you told all your friends to set up blind dates for you? Did you write in your holiday cards that you are open to meeting Mr. or Ms. Right? What about your fellow employees? Do the people in your life know you are open, available, and looking? If not, what are you afraid of? Having to ask? Looking like a loser? Saying "yes" first? Getting rejected? Giving up control? Are you worried the people you date will know you're looking for love? It's an open secret that everyone wants to connect. Don't waste your time pretending otherwise. You're not in high school anymore. It's not the prom. It's real life.

Fearless Dating starts with you. If you value yourself, you understand that you are a gift to anyone you meet. If you go on dates with the hope of making friends, you will be able to act naturally and easily share your essential nature. When you see others as innocent, you will more quickly see the truth of who they are. When you focus on being loving instead of getting love, you will keep making connections and expanding your circle of friends. Sooner or later, one of those friends will introduce you to your future mate—or will turn out to *be* your mate.

And if all this dating stuff scares you to death, enlist a support buddy or two to help you get started. In *Fearless Living*, I introduced the concept of Fearbuster Support Buddies: people who believe in you and will cheer you on through thick and thin. A Support Buddy can discuss your Dating Log answers with you; keep you focused on your intentions; help you reevaluate your top five traits; and remind you of all you have going for yourself with or without a partner. The Support Buddy could be another single person or someone who is married; it doesn't really matter as long as he or she knows you well and has your best interests at heart. I probably don't need to add this, but Mom is usually not the best choice for a Dating Support Buddy, unless she happens to be exceptionally detached and wise.

While I was separated from my husband and waiting for our divorce to be finalized, one of my Support Buddies suggested I meet some men on the Internet. At first I balked. Me? On the Internet? The type of guys I would date wouldn't be on the Internet. Isn't that for losers who can't get a date? The word *losers* tipped me off: that was fear talking. I knew it was lying to me once again in order to keep me safe, stuck, and alone. Fearlessly, I hopped on the Net with the express purpose of getting back in the saddle. I wanted to practice dating. That's it. Not find love. Not find meaning. Not find my type. Not find chemistry. Just practice.

I sent in my photo and listed my wants on a popular site, and the offers came rolling in. Within a week I had a ton of possible dates. I carefully read each of their e-mails and profiles, searching for signs of my top five qualities rather than checking out if they were my type. I came up with eighteen potentials. I e-mailed back and forth with all eighteen and from that correspondence was able to narrow the field to eight. I dated all eight men and had a great time with each one. In the past, some would never have passed my rigid type test. That simple experiment on the Net pushed me beyond typecasting and opened a new array of possibilities. The screening process kept me safe and increased my chances of making a friend or two. I didn't fall in love, but I gained enough confidence so that the world of men started to look welcoming again.

Sometimes I work with clients who have been out of circulation for a long time or feel extremely uncomfortable making small talk or flirting. I ask them to start with the basics. Make eye contact with a stranger or two (of the opposite sex) per day. Smile. Say hello. Those three skills are vital to building your self-confidence so you can stretch past your comfort zone and find love. When you feel more at ease with the basics, you can move on to small talk. If the thought of chatting with someone new makes you sweat, practice being more yourself with the people in your life who already love you. Then try to have a brief conversation—just a sentence or two—with one stranger a day. Slowly but surely, you will build a solid foundation that will keep expanding with every tool you master.

I have been divorced for several years now and have yet to meet my next husband, but I believe with my whole heart that someday I will. I use dating as an opportunity to practice being the person I want to be in my next marriage. Even if a man isn't all I had hoped for, I'm not bothered because regardless of the outcome, I'm practicing. I'm practicing leaving my fears behind. I'm practicing expressing my feelings but not being run by them. I'm practicing saying "yes" when I want to say "yes" and "no" when "no" is my final answer. And the more I practice, the more prepared I will be when we do meet. That goes for chemistry, too. I'm still more than willing to feel passionate. However, I've got those top five traits locked in my brain and they will always matter more to me than chemistry, no matter how strong its pull. Because the bottom line is, a relationship does not define me. I do.

Truth 6

"Yes" Means Nothing If
You Can't Say "No"

Relationships are where you discover who you are. They push you to the limit, let you see yourself like never before, and help you define what matters most. They can bring out the best and the worst in you for the same reason: you finally feel safe. You relax enough to let your essential nature shine through, and you risk enough to heal the pains of the past.

Yet the paradox is that when you begin to feel safe, you can also begin to act out the fears you have unconsciously acquired from your parents, past loves, and life in general. These fears have been holding you back from true intimacy, and by acting them out you are instinctively trying to heal them. A fear of rejection may manifest itself by making you appear extra needy. A fear of being hurt could show up as unrealistic demands placed upon your mate to force him to keep proving he loves you. If you fear a loss of independence, you might feel claustrophobic after spending two days in a row with your significant other. To heal your fears, you secretly pray that this time the other person will love you enough not to leave but instead help you work through it.

Of course, the sole purpose of a relationship is not to heal your past fears, but this healing process is a natural benefit of a loving relationship. Healthy relationships heal because love heals. You heal because you learn to love yourself through every conflict. And through conflicts, you find out what your boundaries are.

Each time you and your partner stumble into a boundary conflict, you have to answer the Big Three relationship questions: Who am I? Who are you? What are we together? Each time you agree on a new boundary, you commit to the relationship all over again. Setting boundaries is how you build the love and intimacy you crave. You learn how to say "yes" and really mean it only when you feel confident and strong enough to say "no."

Safety Lies in Boundaries

For most people, feeling safe begins with having the courage to set boundaries. Very few people like the word *boundary*. I used to dislike it myself. When it came to discussing love, I wanted a warm and fuzzy word that didn't sound so harsh, cold, and real. Yet when someone is crossing your boundary, that is exactly what it feels like. Harsh, cold, and real. I realized I couldn't ignore or improve on the word *boundary*. The fact is, most conflicts between two people involve someone feeling as if his or her boundary has been violated. It comes out as, "You don't respect me," "You're trying to tell me what to do," or, "None of your business," but the underlying message is the same: You have crossed a line.

A simple definition of "knowing your boundaries" is the ability to distinguish your own feelings, fears, and responsibilities from someone else's. A boundary breaker may not see the two of you as separate individuals. The line where you end and he or she begins may be blurred. Therefore, it is up to you to become vigilant about understanding what your boundaries are and how they affect your self-esteem.

Setting boundaries is vital to the survival of any relationship. Each time the need for a boundary arises, it points to a problem that is brewing. When you put a boundary in place, you are saying you care enough about yourself and your mate to work through the problem. By talking to your partner about whatever has made you feel threatened or destabilized, you can make your way back to safety with your relationship not only intact but stronger.

Boundaries not only make you feel safe, they make the people you love feel safe as well. When you are clear about your boundaries and know how to express them, your loved ones can relax. They don't have to worry about crossing some line you have never told them about. They don't need to walk on eggshells around you or wonder if you resent them for a boundary they violated last week or last year. If you have children, it is urgent that you raise them in a household where people know their boundaries and can freely talk about them. They cannot learn this on their own! I don't think I am exaggerating when I say that teaching your children about boundaries is the most loving and valuable gift you will ever give them.

Setting boundaries will also remind you of your original intention to love fearlessly. You will reawaken your commitment to love yourself, which will increase your self-respect. I have occasionally had to choose between setting a personal boundary and giving up a relationship. Making that choice, I had to face my fears. Sometimes that meant I had to face my feelings of being wrong, stupid, or rejected. Each time I rose to the challenge by being true to myself, it made me stretch. It made me discover who I was and what I valued.

I have learned firsthand that without clear boundaries, love becomes stifling. "Stand together yet not too near together," wrote Kahlil Gibran. "The oak tree and the cypress grow not in each other's shadow." Without boundaries, love changes from a celebration of each other's individuality to a web of mutual dependency. Without boundaries, one person can get lost in the other, or they can both get lost in the false security of codependency. Instead of being a creative force, the relationship drains both people's strength and passion. Instead of generating more love, the relationship generates fear.

In the rest of this chapter I will share what I have discovered about boundaries in my own life and from coaching couples. As you move through a relationship—from casual dating, to a serious commitment, and on through marriage and long-term love—you will see how some boundaries shift while others remain firm. You will learn when to draw a line in the sand and how to choose your battles. You will discover how to recognize when others are violating your boundaries and when you are violating theirs. You will begin to understand the difference between neediness and love, support and sacrifice, commitment and manipulation. I will show you how making your way through these complex emotions gets easier if you follow three fearless principles:

- Honor your essential nature

- Stay compassionate

- Stand for your truth

These guiding principles will help two committed people through the most difficult of times and, if need be, they will show you how to get out of a dangerous relationship with your self-esteem intact.

Your Boundaries or Your Life

Eric and I met through mutual friends. "He's the perfect guy for you, Rhonda," they gushed. "Successful, handsome, athletic, and spiritual." An incredible combination, for sure. I wasn't feeling particularly attractive or ready for romance, but I knew love doesn't wait until you're ready, so I accepted Eric's invitation for an afternoon latte.

He was just under six feet, with wavy black hair and sharp blue eyes. You could tell he took care of himself by the way he moved and how well his clothes fit him.Settling into a deep, upholstered chair at the café, he stretched his legs out in front of him as if he owned the place. As we talked, Eric seemed too good to be true. We appeared to be compatible in every sense of the word. I immediately put on my caution hat. Part of me was completely infatuated with him, while the other part wondered if he wasn't putting on an act. I figured it would become clear during our first three dates. I was willing to wait.

After three dates, I could see Eric did have some desirable qualities. One in particular stood out: his doggone persistence. He wanted me and let me know it, wooing me like nobody had ever done before. The more I shared my dreams and desires, the more he used that information to try to make me happy. I was in heaven.

Within a month he had pledged his undying love. But did I love him? I certainly wasn't ready to do anything rash, such as give in to love just because he loved me. I needed to know that I really loved him. To test the waters, I began to introduce him to my world. My friends liked him. My dogs licked him hello. Everyone who met him thought we were meant for each other. *We are a good couple,* I thought. *He is good to me.*

Eric courted me for three months before I finally had to agree, this was love. With our commitment firmly in place, we spent the night together. As much as I desired Eric, there was no way I could have imagined what happened that first evening. It was as if he wanted to devour me. No one had ever wanted me so intensely or fulfilled me so well. But just as we were about to consummate our love, I hesitated. I couldn't go through with it. I wasn't ready for this next phase of commitment. As he leaned in to kiss me, I whispered in his ear, "I'm not ready." He sat straight up, his legs straddled around my waist, and said calmly and clearly, "You cannot deny me."

Every cell in my body froze. This felt wrong. But all I could think about was how much he loved me and how just that afternoon I had told him I loved him, too. *What's the big deal, Rhonda? Just let the guy make love to you.* And so I did. It was the most incredible night of lovemaking in my life, but I had no idea how that decision, that seemingly minor self-betrayal, would determine the fate of our relationship.

As we approached the six-month mark, Eric started to go through some difficult times. His company was talking about layoffs, and he had only recently been hired. I knew things weren't looking good for him. He became moody and needed more attention, but I figured I had seen the "real" Eric and this was just him under stress, nothing time wouldn't heal. I told myself that the minute Eric felt more secure at work all would be right again. I knew we could get through this if I was just patient, understanding, and focused on his needs.

But as six months became eight, Eric began to show a side I hadn't seen. He asked to see my financials, and in order to make him feel secure, I reluctantly agreed. I thought this would prove once and for all that I loved him. Instead, he started figuring out how I could support him if he lost his job. He would look over my shoulder when I was writing and question my ideas and my writing style. Sometimes he would tell me to remove passages he didn't like. Making love was now a manly conquest. It was no longer fun and relaxing but more like a competitive sport. One orgasm wasn't enough for him; he wanted to break every record, whether or not I was interested. He became jealous of my friends and wanted to know who I was with whenever I went out. He began to point out things he didn't like about me that he had once claimed to love. Still, I chalked his behavior up to the stress he was under. I racked my brain for solutions, yet no matter what I tried, things continued to get worse. It seemed I couldn't do anything right.

I didn't know which reality to believe anymore. When I was away from Eric, I missed him terribly. When I was with him, I just wanted to get away. The love that I couldn't get enough of was beginning to feel suffocating. *Maybe it is me*, I thought. *I just have to try harder.* But regardless of how hard I tried to keep him happy, he never returned to being good ol' Eric. Each day my self-confidence slipped a little further. I began to doubt my intuition and my sanity. Was I abnormal? Unworthy of him? Unable to love? I was in too deep to tell.

It was as if Eric wanted me to trust him more than I trusted myself, to depend on him exclusively. Yet no matter how I trusted him, how often we spoke (he called me at least ten times a day), how intense the sex, there was no satisfying him. His jealousy only grew and, although I couldn't bear to admit it, he seemed to be developing a mean streak. I did finally admit to myself that our relationship was making me feel crazy. And I couldn't ignore the fact that my father had always made me feel crazy, too. My father had never listened, only lectured. He had put me down even when I was an "A" student. Nothing I did was good enough for him, and after trying to please him to no avail, I eventually gave up.

I didn't want to give up on Eric, but each time he accused me of something I hadn't done, I knew this couldn't go on. I was at my wit's end. Then one evening, as we were sitting in front of the fireplace, he looked over at me with a slightly disgusted expression and said, "Boy, are you getting fat. You sure are lucky to have me, because you aren't going to get any better looking. And honey, I love you just the way you are."

The words were so hostile that for a minute I thought he must be joking. He wasn't. It kept happening again and again over the next few weeks. Eric told me that I was fat and that my breasts were shrinking. He reminded me how lucky I was to have him since I was getting older. I told him that talking to me that way wasn't making me love him more, it was making me love him less. It had no effect on him.

Through all of this, I refused to admit that Eric was emotionally abusive. Like most victims of verbal abuse, I began to justify his behavior. It was true, I *had* gained a few pounds and I *was* getting older. Everything he pointed out did have a tiny kernel of truth in it. And when he was good, he was so good. In the beginning it had been the most loving relationship I had ever experienced. But when he was bad? It was by far the least loving I had encountered, except, of course, for my father. *Maybe this is how most men are*, I thought. *What if this is as good as I deserve?* I wanted to minimize his current behavior, deny how I was feeling, and ignore what was happening. I started to doubt myself. *Maybe the good is worth the bad?*

For two more months, I battled Eric and my fears of being alone, a loser, and worthless. I was exhausted. Fear will use every tool you have, every device, every gesture, every motion, every word, against you. Fear kept telling me that if I left Eric it would prove that my father was right, that I was unlovable. But if could just get Eric to change, I would finally have the evidence to prove my father wrong: I was worthy of love. Fear whispered, *You aren't working hard enough. You should know how to solve this. Aren't you the coach?*

By now Eric was talking marriage. I knew in my heart that if I went through with it I was in for a repeat of my mother's life. Yet I was afraid of what he might do if I just left him cold. He constantly told me that if I ever left him, life wouldn't be worth living, which fed my fears that one more person who loved me was going to die. I stayed. I waited. I tried to please him. I even went to therapy with him. But I had forgotten one thing: I had betrayed myself. In the moment I said yes when I wanted to say no, the stage was set. I had allowed Eric to manipulate me and now I was giving up on myself in order to be loved.

But if I gave up on me, who was he in love with?

I called Marta and told her that I didn't feel like empowered, optimistic Rhonda. She confessed that I hadn't been acting like myself, either. I asked her to help me and she gently pointed out the ways in which my mood had changed. Never did she mention Eric, but I could see the pattern. Each time I was with him, I got emotionally beaten up. Instead of standing up for myself I lay there and took the beating, then vented my pain and anger on my friends. I was losing myself in Eric, and I had to get some space to find me again. Fear was in charge and choosing my reactions. I had lost control.

The next day I tried to tell him that I needed some time to think about us. He became eerily quiet. I cautiously mentioned that he had talked about visiting his family, and maybe this was a good time. He walked out of the room. I followed him like a puppy dog, trying to get him to agree to take a two-week vacation without me. "That's all I need," I assured him. "It's all *we* need." He walked outside. I decided it was best to leave him alone to think about it.

A few minutes later he came back in the room. "I am not going anywhere without you," he informed me, his voice like ice. "How dare you think you can make it on your own. I gave you everything, and this is how you show your appreciation? I love you too much, Rhonda, to let this happen. *You owe me.* Your friends warned me about you. They told me you would do this. They told me you're ungrateful and not worth all the trouble I've been going through. You disgust me, Rhonda. You're a user and a slut."

And on he went, for three hours. He called me names and told me I had betrayed him, lied to him, and led him on. Every few minutes he kept repeating, "Can't you see I love you?" It was then that I *knew* I had to leave.

Knowing you need to leave someone and actually doing it can be miles apart. I had to admit to myself that I was in love with Eric mostly because I was afraid of the alternative. I was afraid to be alone. I was afraid to admit that I couldn't fix him or solve our problems. I was afraid to admit that I felt worthless. I was staying with him out of fear and calling it love.

Eric's brand of love came at a price, and that price was my self-esteem. I was stunned when I realized how much I had given up. As the affair began to implode, I wrote in my journal:

My father kept repeating that he loved my mother.
Eric keeps telling me he loves me.
My father begged her for another chance.
Eric wants another chance.
My mother wanted to believe him.
So do I.

My mother took him back.
I must not. I cannot.

That is the voice of a woman who has lost sight of her boundaries and is fighting for her life. I never want it to happen to you.

Basic Boundaries for You and Your Partner

In a healthy, loving household, children learn boundaries naturally. Through interactions with their parents and family, they internalize the self-esteem that enables them to say no, walk away from dangerous or damaging situations, express themselves assertively, keep secrets without guilt, and stand up for themselves even if they have to stand alone. When all those pieces of self-esteem are present, it is clear when a boundary needs to be put in place with a mate, friend, or stranger.

In reality, many of us did not grow up with all those pieces intact. Setting boundaries doesn't come so naturally to us, as I found out the hard way with Eric. These days, when I am teaching my clients about Fearless Loving, I offer them my definition of healthy boundaries for couples. I explain that boundaries can encompass your physical space, your personal space, your body, and the way you communicate with each other. The intention in Fearless Loving is to honor your boundaries without dishonoring your partner's. Never make your needs more important than the other person's, yet recognize when your needs are mandatory in order to continue feeling safe and respected in the relationship. Boundaries are not about building barricades to love or putting someone through the twelve Labors of Hercules to prove they care. Boundaries are about honoring the soul in front of you.

Statistically, boundary-breakers are male. The are most often the aggressors in domestic violence disputes. Yet countless women violate boundaries and use other forms of emotional abuse to feel in control. Regardless of what sex you are, boundaries are boundaries. Abuse is abuse. The examples in this chapter reflect the most common stories I have encountered; therefore the boundary breaker is usually a man. But I recognize that boundary abuse knows no gender, and there are men out there who have suffered just as much as women.

In all relationships, some boundaries are ironclad and others are more flexible. The bottom line is, what are the issues you will never compromise? Those combine to form your line in the sand, which you will protect even if it means breaking up. Everything else can be negotiated, and those negotiations are the way a healthy relationship evolves.

There are certain boundaries I believe everyone must protect. Being aware of these boundaries may be your salvation if you find yourself involved with a man or woman who becomes controlling, manipulative, or abusive.

☀ Fearbuster Exercise: ☀ Boundary Checklist

Place a check mark next to the boundary violation if it has happened to you.

Basic Boundaries: You May Not . . .

_____ Call me names

_____ Ridicule or belittle me in private or public

_____ Lie to me

_____ Hit me or physically hurt me in any way

_____ Be unfaithful to me

_____ Spy on me

_____ Say things that are purposely designed to make me doubt whether I am sane or normal

_____ Use traumas in my past to emotionally manipulate me

_____ Pressure me to cut ties with my family or friends

_____ Stonewall me—refuse to communicate

_____ Undermine me at my work or with my family or friends

_____ Attempt to turn my children against me

_____ Hurt my children in any way: physically, sexually, or mentally

_____ Be overly critical, implying I don't do anything right

_____ Force me to have sex when I don't want to

_____ Blame me for the state of your life

_____ Intimidate or threaten me

These are the core elements of healthy boundaries. People who violate them are potential abusers or are currently abusing you.

You might even be surprised to identify yourself as a boundary-breaker after you read the above list. Awareness is the first step toward taking responsibility for your actions.

And let's get something straight right away: Abusers never have to touch you physically. Eric didn't. He ripped me up from the inside out. Physical and emotional abuse are fueled by the same fears, they just leave different scars.

When you are on your Wheel of Fear you may very well try to rationalize your mate's behavior, as I did with Eric. My fear kept telling me that this wasn't the "real" Eric, that his behavior wasn't out of the ordinary, that maybe I was to blame. Eric agreed, of course. As far as he was concerned, there was nothing wrong with him. He would say he was sorry after he yelled at me. He would cry when I cried. He would go to therapy sessions under the guise of getting help, but it didn't help. Instead, he'd use the sessions to gather evidence about how right he was and how wrong I was. The anger management classes he attended just made him a smarter abuser. They didn't stop his behavior because he truly believed he did not have a problem.

And I had to face that I was to blame for *accepting* his behavior toward me. I had refused to listen to my intuition. I had refused to stand for myself. I had refused to cut the relationship off when I could see where it was heading, all because I wanted to be right about Eric. However, that did not mean I caused his abuse. I did nothing to deserve being treated in that manner.

Abusers can be very sophisticated in defense of their own actions. In their minds, it is never their fault. They want you to believe that if you would only hear better, care more, or be different, things would change. But I have learned the truth. You are not to blame. You are not crazy, stupid, or too sensitive. And if anyone says you are, *leave*! People usually hang in there in an effort to understand why this is happening to them, so they can feel better about their choices. But haven't you tried? You've stood by him, right? Standing by someone only works if he truly wants to change. He must ask for help. He must take responsibility for his actions. Once he can see how his own fears trick him into blaming you, your partner might have a chance to change. But let me warn you, do not attempt this alone. Get help from a qualified therapist who can help you clarify your boundaries and find yourself again.

Maintaining your physical and emotional well-being is boundary number one. Protecting yourself from people who might violate that boundary is a main component of the dating plan I described in the last chapter. You'll recall that I asked you to change something—time, day, location—on one of your dates so you can tell how flexible the other person is, how willing to share control. The time limits for the first few dates are there for the same reason: to see whether the other person will accept your limit or try to change your mind. It is a litmus test for potential boundary-breakers. In his outstanding book *The Gift of Fear: Survival Signals That Protect Us from Violence*, Gavin de Becker explains that "declining to hear 'no' is a signal that someone is either seeking control or refusing to relinquish it . . . never, ever, relent on the issue of 'no,' because it sets the stage for more efforts to control." Do not repeat my mistake. Eric did not accept "no," I acquiesced, and eventually he became abusive. If your date can accept "no" and is flexible, it does not guarantee that he or she won't someday become abusive, but it brings the likelihood down.

What if you are already involved with someone whose behavior makes you feel bad but who has managed to convince you that it's your problem? Boundaries must be put in place immediately if you sense that your partner is using any of the following tactics to control you.

Fearbuster Exercise:
Are You Being Emotionally Abused?

Ask yourself if you feel . . .

Blamed. You blame yourself and your mate does the same. Everything, including his or her life, is your fault.

Criticized. Your partner has convinced you his or her way is always better. You feel as if you can't do anything right. You might think, "What is wrong with me?" or, "Why can't I make anything work?" You begin to doubt your abilities, thoughts, and feelings.

Powerless/Helpless/Trapped. You feel as if you have no way out. Perhaps he controls the checkbook or some other aspect of your life. He won't listen or change his behavior. You want to have some personal control but instead you have no say.

Humiliated. He or she laughs at you, scorns you, and generally ridicules you. Name calling, put-downs, and sarcasm are used to make you feel powerless.

Intimidated. Your partner need only glance at you to stop you in your tracks. He or she walks toward you in a threatening way or raises his or her fists in anger. You shut up, shut down, and attempt to keep small to stay safe.

Threatened. Your partner claims to know all about you. He or she threatens to tell everyone "the truth" about you, and that could include spreading lies.

Isolated. Your partner insists on spending every minute with you. At first it feels flattering, later it feels confining. Your partner tries to convince you to see less of your friends and family and spend all your time with him or her.

Owned. You partner claims to own you, insists that the two of you are merged, that you are nothing without him or her, that you will never find someone else to love you as well—or to love you at all.

Dirty/Ugly/Ashamed. He uses sex as a weapon to overcome his lack of control. He pressures or forces you to have sex but blames you for the outcome or claims that you like it. He tells you that if you were different, things would be better.

Crazy. Your partner calls you crazy, weird, a loser, incompetent, or any other name intended to make you doubt your sanity or intuition. Abusers want to control not only your physical whereabouts but also your mind. They want you to doubt yourself so you rely solely on them. You may wonder if you are actually going crazy.

Depressed/Hopeless. Each day feels harder than the last. It feels as if there is no way out of your relationship. Your motto has become, "What's the use?"

If you see yourself in any of the above situations, please don't look away. You aren't a bad or stupid person for loving someone who may mistreat you. It happens to the best of us, including me. I was, and am, a confident, successful woman who thought she could see through a man at ten paces. Yet I fell prey to Eric's charms because of my fear of being alone, wrong, and unlovable. Perhaps the person who mistreats you one day makes up for it brilliantly the next, as Eric seemed to. Many people, because of their fears, don't know the difference between authentic, committed love and how fear uses love as its foil.

Two books were especially helpful to me as I was recovering from Eric's "love": *The Verbally Abusive Relationship*, by Patricia Evans, and *The Emotionally Abused Woman* by Beverly Engel. They helped me understand how my thirst for worthiness had overridden my common sense. When my friends mentioned that Eric appeared controlling, I brushed it off and told them he was attentive and caring. His ten phone calls a day just made me feel wanted. I had left a marriage feeling barely desirable, and Eric seemed to be the answer to my prayers for a partner who would cherish me. His jealousy and overprotection, I rationalized, proved that he valued me and wanted to keep me safe.

Your reasons for staying with someone who is abusive are probably different than mine, but they share a common root: *fear*. Although the thought of setting boundaries with this person may terrify you—you may fear, as I did, that if you mess up this relationship you will never be loved again—you must stand up for yourself. There are major consequences for not setting and keeping these basic boundaries:

- You will lose respect for yourself

- Your self-esteem will wither

- After a while, you will stop trusting yourself

- Your abuser will seize on your self-doubt to make you rely more and more on him or her

When that happens, you may begin to lose sight of who you are. You may even come to believe that you *must* lose yourself in order to be loved.

I found out that losing yourself doesn't happen all at once. It's a slow, almost imperceptible process. You start out in a relationship strong and self-assured, then lose your way when small boundary battles start to come up. Maybe your partner can argue you into a corner, and you figure that because he won the argument he gets to be "right." Perhaps she knows how to make you feel sorry for her so that you'll let her have her way, even if it violates your boundary. Maybe he's got a terrible temper and you just don't want to face it. But setting your basic boundaries is not a matter of who's right or wrong, or of letting something slide out of pity or fear. Basic boundaries are nothing less than basic human rights. Stand for them, or risk losing everything.

If It Makes Sense to You, It's a Boundary

If you're involved with someone who is not abusive, the boundary issues you deal with are probably less intense but every bit as anxiety provoking. That's because the boundaries that matter to us often don't make much sense to our partner. That's okay. Your partner will honor your boundaries not because they make sense but because they are yours. And this goes both ways. In fact, honoring your partner's odd, unreasonable, or seemingly silly boundary without questioning it is a very powerful and loving act of acceptance. Think carefully before you say no to a boundary request. Honoring a boundary is an opportunity to practice detachment (by not taking things personally) and acceptance (by loving your mate as is). When you honor his or her request, you are giving a clear signal that you are saying yes to love. The relationship will reap big rewards in good will, trust, and intimacy.

Myrna, forty-three, and Scott, forty-five, had been dating for three years when they decided to marry. Both had lived alone since their early twenties and were nervous about sharing an apartment. "All the advice books say to move into a new place so you'll feel like it belongs to both of you equally," Myrna said. "But Scott's apartment is in the Old Town historical district. It's beautiful, huge, and rent controlled. We'll never find a better deal. The smart thing is for me to move in with him, but I'm afraid he'll want to throw out all my stuff because his is better. I'm worried he won't want to hang my artwork or let my taste show through."

All Myrna's fears crystallized around closet space. The apartment had plenty of closets, but over the years Scott had filled them all up. Although she was afraid Scott would think she was greedy, Myrna stated her boundaries: she would need two-thirds of the closet space all to herself. Not half. More than half. To her surprise, Scott agreed without a fight.

Three months later, when she was all moved in, Myrna confessed that one closet was still empty and Scott hadn't said a word. "I guess I didn't have so much stuff after all. I think the closets were standing in for what I was really afraid of: getting buried under Scott's personality and losing my own voice. I wasn't used to sharing, and felt like it was him or me. Now I have more confidence that it can be him *and* me." By respecting Myrna's boundaries, Scott sent a clear message that he loved her and was willing to give something up in order to make her feel safe. Myrna never told Scott, "I'm afraid I'll lose myself when I move in with you," but she didn't have to.

I've noticed that when people start setting boundaries for the first time they often overcompensate, as Myrna did. She asked for more than enough to make sure she got what she needed. That is normal. You might also discover, to your dismay, that when you ask for a boundary it comes out sounding shrill and demanding rather than loving. Again, this is normal. You are finding your own power. To soften the request, you might want to preface it with, "I'm new at this boundary thing so it may not come out right, but I need . . ." That helps the other person listen to the request instead of turning off to your tone.

Personal boundaries like Myrna's closet space are often responses to a fear that your partner is going to tread on your territory in an especially sensitive area. As Myrna put it, the boundaries "stand in" for bigger issues. Here are a few boundaries my clients have set, followed by the fears that motivated them.

- I must play soccer with my buddies every Saturday. (I'm afraid you'll want me to stop seeing my friends.)

- I must have a cleaning lady twice a month. (I'm afraid you'll take me for granted.)

- I must visit my mother for one week every summer. (I'm afraid you won't honor my relationship with my mother.)

- The children must go to Sunday school. (I'm afraid you don't think religion is important.)

- I must go out to dinner with my girlfriends one night a week. (I'm afraid you will become too protective and jealous.)

- I must have my own checking account with my own money in it that I am free to spend as I choose. (I'm afraid you will control the money, treat me like a child, and give me no say.)

- We must have a date night once a week. (I'm afraid you'll see me only as a mother instead of the sexy woman you married.)

- We must go away on a vacation at least once a year to someplace other than our parents'. (I'm afraid we'll become all work and no play.)

- You must call me if you are going to be late from work. (I'm afraid you don't care about me enough or think I'm too dependent if I call you.)

The woman who wanted to go out with her girlfriends every week was healing her fears about being controlled by putting a boundary in place. She made her request clear and stuck to it. Her husband didn't particularly like being left to his own devices one night a week, and he groused about it now and then, but to her it was nonnegotiable. She wanted a sense of independence and this was her way of claiming her power.

Boundaries such as "The children must go to Sunday school," are more complicated. When a couple first starts getting serious, these are the types of things that may cause conflict and consequently get swept under the rug. "Who knows if we'll even have kids? It's way too early to talk about Sunday school." It's easy to let a boundary issue slide for the sake of keeping the peace. "I've told him how I feel and he heard me," you may think. "If he cares about me, he'll choose the behavior that pleases me." But how do you know? What if he doesn't understand how much you care about it? What if he doesn't see it the same way? Never let an issue slide if it is important to you. You don't necessarily need to resolve it, but you do need to clearly state your boundary by saying something such as, "I know for sure that if we ever do have children, I will want to join a church and send them to Sunday school. I feel very strongly about it, and I know that won't change." State your truth now, so that if it comes up later your partner won't be surprised by your commitment.

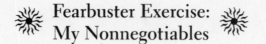 Fearbuster Exercise: My Nonnegotiables

What areas of your life are nonnegotiable? What must occur in order for you to feel safe enough to love, grow, and be yourself? These areas are your "must-have" boundary list. They don't have to be big issues, but if you can't think of anything at all, you may not be standing up for yourself as much as you could. These are the areas of your life where you can begin to practice being the fearless you.

Ask yourself: Are you honoring your essential nature? Staying compassionate with yourself and others? Standing for your truth regardless of other people's opinions? If you answer no to any of those questions, putting a boundary in place will help you get back to your center and love yourself more fearlessly.

In order to set appropriate boundaries, think about what you would need in your relationship in order to feel respected. What is reasonable? What is causing havoc in your life? What would make you feel better? Be truthful. There may be something simple that would make all the difference in the world if you communicated your request.

In each of the following areas, write down your "must-have" boundaries:

Career:

Romance:

Communication:

Children:

Home:

Friends:

Fun:

Hobbies:

Vacations:

Health:

Hey, I Didn't Know I Had that Boundary

Even if we think carefully about our boundaries and try to figure out what they are, the fact is we often don't know we have a
boundary until someone violates it. That's what happened to Doug,
who couldn't understand why he resented his girlfriend. "When
Candace comes over to spend the night, the first night is fine, but
the next one and each night after that gets worse. I start feeling
restless, I can't sleep, and I can't relax. It gets to the point where I
become mad and start yelling at her. What's wrong with me?"

"Nothing," I told him. "You're just afraid to put boundaries in
place. Your fear of being seen as unlovable has convinced you that
love means never saying no, so you get angry with her when you
want to say no and can't."

Doug believed that if you love someone you should want to be
around her as much as possible, and he assumed Candace felt the
same way. He was afraid she would think he was rejecting her if he
asked her not to spend the night. On a deeper level, Doug feared
that maybe he really *didn't* love Candace since he seemed only to
want her around one night at a time. Doug's fear-based—and unconscious—solution was to let Candace spend one night at his
place, then get crabbier and crabbier until she finally gave up and
went home.

I advised Doug to begin again. "Tell her that you have finally figured out why you sometimes get so grumpy with her. Explain that you need time alone to appreciate her, rejuvenate, and be present with her. Let her know that from now on you would love her to spend one night a week at your apartment, but no more unless you both agree to it. And then stick to your plan."

Doug hadn't realized that he was getting angry with Candace because of his own inability to set boundaries, but now that he knew, it was up to him to do something about it. He would only be setting himself up for more frustration and guilt if he ignored his need for personal space. It was true that Candace might disagree with him or get her feelings hurt, but that was a risk Doug had to take. If she loved him, she would understand and respect his request, even if it hurt. If she was not interested in what his needs were, she didn't love him *no matter what she said.* Actions speak louder than words, especially when it comes to honoring someone's boundaries.

"The same goes for you," I told Doug. "Your actions reflect who you are. Be consistent. Be firm. No defending yourself, counterattacking, or seeking Candace's approval for your boundaries. As you take care of yourself, you will be able to communicate more clearly and love more deeply."

How can you recognize if someone has crossed a boundary you didn't know you had? It's easy once you know the signs. Your body tells you, your behavior tells you, and your feelings tell you. Physical signs that someone is violating your boundary might include stomach cramps, a headache, or back pain. Those are the most common sites that react to psychological stress, but yours might be different. We all have a spot that starts hurting when things get tense—you know what yours is.

Your behavior can also tell you when your boundary is being violated. This may include being irritable, jealous, critical, or judgmental; forgetting dates; forgetting to bring contraception so that you can't have sex or are forced into an argument about it; stonewalling communication; walking out.

Feelings that arise within you also point to boundary violations. They can include anger, resentment, lack of sexual desire, shutting down, depression, panic, helplessness, confusion, disconnectedness, frustration, and feeling off-balance or invisible.

In any relationship it is normal to have *some* of these feelings and physical reactions and to behave badly or forget things *some* of the time. The way to tell if it's related to a boundary violation is to look for a pattern. Doug always got irritable by the second night Candace stayed over. I always snapped at Marta after I had been with Eric. To an outsider the connection may seem obvious, but when you're inside the relationship fears can cloud your perceptions. Notice when the feelings, behavior, or physical distress is occurring, and remember that the boundary doesn't need to seem fair or make sense to anyone but you. You can still request it, talk about it, and find out how the other person feels. If he or she is a potential abuser, there is little that talking will do—professional help is the answer. If you are with someone who truly wants to work on loving you fearlessly, his or her response may surprise you and the conversation will make you closer.

Dating and Boundaries

The boundaries you establish at the beginning of a relationship set the tone for all the years to come. That's not to say you can't change boundaries once you are deep into a relationship. You can, but it takes much more effort and commitment. In the beginning, the person who continues to violate your boundaries—even seemingly small ones—is giving you vital information about his or her character. This person is attempting to wear you down. If you let him or her succeed, prepare to be manipulated, controlled, and blamed for the entire duration of your relationship.

Gail, a middle-school teacher, had a terrible problem with time management. She was late for everything. Each day she would rush into her classroom as the bell was ringing, looking more frazzled than her fourteen-year-old students. But it was her personal relationships that really suffered because of her chronic tardiness. "My best friend always gives me fake times," Gail confessed. "If we're meeting for a one o'clock movie, she'll say it starts at twelve. Sometimes it works. She puts up with me, but other people get really mad. I want to change."

Making people wait is usually a sign that the late person feels inadequate in some way. I once read that Marilyn Monroe was often late for work (and just about everything else) because she loved to soak in the bathtub imagining all those people waiting for her. It made her feel special to know that no matter how angry they got, she was such a big star that they *had* to wait. In Gail's case, the tardiness was directly related to her fear of rejection. By being late, she was rejecting the other person first, using manipulation to make him work harder on the relationship than she was, and acting overscheduled so she would seem important.

When Gail met Martin, she thought he might be someone special. "He's that compact, wiry type of guy that really turns me on. He owns a furniture restoration business, and in his spare time he designs his own furniture. It's gorgeous." But old habits are hard to break, and on her second date with Martin, Gail was twenty-five minutes late. Unlike most men, who either fumed silently or gave her hell for her tardiness, Martin simply refused to accept it. "I want to date someone who will treat me with respect," he told her calmly, kindly, and without judgment. "If you're always going to be late, I don't think this will work for me."

When men shouted at her or seethed and sulked, Gail could chalk it up to their impatience or tell herself they didn't really care for her. She could blame them instead of acknowledging that she was the source of the problem. Martin, however, was not attacking her the way the others had. He had merely put a boundary in place. She could either respect it or they would not date—not because she was a bad person but because they did not have the same values. He was vulnerable enough to admit that her lateness made him feel bad, and he liked himself enough not to allow her to treat him poorly. It made Martin even more attractive to Gail, who realized that she very much wanted to continue to see him.

Instinctively, Martin knew that Gail would need a little time to process the boundary he had drawn. He stated his case in a detached and friendly way, then backed off and let the information sink in while they shared a pleasant meal together. At the end of it, Gail apologized and promised to be more sensitive about time. Because Martin had not reacted in anger, there was no need for her to defend herself. He gave her the emotional space she needed to gain insight into her behavior without feeling as if she had lost face.

Saying the Hard Words: A Strategy for Setting Boundaries

When I tell clients they need to set some boundaries, they usually react as if I've offered them a plate of burned cookies. I understand. Setting boundaries always means rocking the boat, and most people have a hard time with that. "I know I need to set boundaries," they'll agree. "I want to set them, but . . ."

"He already thinks I'm high-maintenance, and I don't want to ask for anything more."

"She takes everything so personally, she'll just think I'm criticizing her."

"The last time I tried to talk to him about boundaries, he laughed at my 'psychobabble' and accused me of turning everything into work."

"She'll say I'm too sensitive and ignore my request, as usual."

Some of these worries are based on previous experience, others are unsubstantiated fears. But I have found that it is not uncommon for the person on the receiving end of boundaries to get defensive and have a knee-jerk reaction against them. They'll accuse the boundary-seeker of being crazy, selfish, wrong, or obsessive. It's easy to start doubting yourself when you hear these names directed at you, and self-doubt is the main reason people fail to stick to their boundaries. They feel guilty and ashamed for suggesting the boundary in the first place, and rather than risk more ridicule or a confrontation, they retreat.

It may help to remind yourself and your partner that setting boundaries isn't something you do *to* each other, it is something you agree upon together. The process usually opens up communication about a subject that was taboo, ignored, or avoided in the past. By bringing up the issue, you accept responsibility for your part in it—your feelings, fears, and ideas for resolving the conflict and moving past it.

Don't be surprised if, after you've agreed upon a boundary, it doesn't quite work out or needs to be tweaked. Sometimes the process of figuring out a boundary clarifies the issue, and the need for it dissolves. You don't even need to use the word *boundary* when you are expressing your request. Just stating what you need may be enough.

After setting a boundary and going through the process of standing for it, you may discover that the boundary you thought you cared about wasn't really the issue at all. You may find out that it is something much deeper or very different than what you suspected. But learning to stand for one boundary will give you the tools to deal more effectively with any issue between the two of you. Each time a boundary is set, the people involved are learning about themselves and each other, and intimacy grows.

Boundary-Maker and Boundary-Breaker

The following five-step strategy works well for people who have trouble setting and keeping boundaries. Once you try it you'll see that the process can be civil, safe, and liberating for both partners.

Step One: Choose Your Battles

Whenever a conflict flares up in your relationship, rate the issue from 1 to 10 (10 being the most challenging, difficult, frustrating conflicts). If it is less than a 5, either work out a solution with your mate quickly or let it go. If it is 5 to 7, think about frequency and impact. How often does the issue come up? What happens when it does? Who is affected? If you truly cannot continue without resolving it, go ahead to Step Two. If it is irritating but manageable, consider letting it go for a month and seeing how you feel. Sometimes things resolve themselves if you give them a chance. If the issue rates an 8 to a 10, I encourage you to deal with it right away.

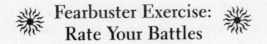

Fearbuster Exercise: Rate Your Battles

Name your top three boundary violators. It could be your mate, but it doesn't have to be. Your mother, your boss, a friend, or anyone else will do. When you learn how to set boundaries with one person, it will become easier to set them with your partner. If you are not completely sure whether the person is violating your boundary, write it down anyway. You are just practicing. After each name, describe the situation. How does the boundary usually get violated? Next, rate the violation 1 through 10. Last, write down your boundary request. If you need help, refer to page 165 for a refresher on nonnegotiables.

Violator One:

Situation:

Rating:

Boundary request:

Violator Two:

Situation:

Rating:

Boundary request:

Violator Three:

Situation:

Rating:

Boundary request:

If you have more than one violation that rates 5 or higher, pick the one that would either give you an immediate sense of relief or is the easiest to deal with. I understand they all may look hard. But setting a boundary with a new date is less risky than doing it with someone who activates your fears day in and day out.

Step Two: Know Your Motivation

Before you discuss the boundary with the other person, ask yourself what you want to achieve by putting it in place. For example, if you are setting the boundary with your partner and the result you are looking for is, "I will know he loves me," you may be using the boundary only as a love test. If you want to be in better health, get more sleep, improve your lot at work, or some other goal that relates to your sense of self, the boundary is probably reasonable. "Don't tease me in front of my boss" is a reasonable boundary request. "Stop spending Wednesday night with your brothers and stay home with me," may not be so reasonable.

Many times I find that people set boundaries because they don't want to get hurt. One woman told me that her boyfriend had stopped phoning her for a week. When he finally called, he said he needed some time to think about their relationship. She blew up. "You're triggering my abandonment issues! You can't violate my boundaries like that."

"So he doesn't get to process his feelings, only you do?" I asked her. "This isn't about boundaries. You have a fear of abandonment regardless of him. Making him responsible for these fears is making his needs inconsequential. Besides, you can't make him stay if he doesn't want to by calling it a boundary issue."

A more reasonable way to deal with her fear of abandonment would be to ask her boyfriend to tell her when he needed time alone rather than just disappearing, and to let her know when he feels fearful rather than hiding those feelings. I also advised her to wait until she was calmer to share her feelings, and to make sure it was a good time for him as well. Using boundaries, he can have his process, she can have hers, and they will still be respecting each other's needs.

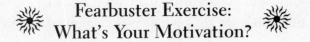

Fearbuster Exercise: What's Your Motivation?

Choose the one person from your top three whom you would like to focus on for the sake of this exercise. Then answer the following question:

Does the boundary you would like to put in place relate only to this person, or to anyone?

If it relates only to this person, it may be saying more about your fears than his or her behavior. If you want to feel special, putting a boundary in place is not the answer. A boundary is set to avoid violation of personal freedoms. It is not a tool to test someone's love. A reasonable boundary is important regardless of the status of the relationship. If someone calls you names, it doesn't matter whether he or she is a stranger or a lover. It is unacceptable.

Step Three: Be Realistic about Your Partner's Abilities

Some boundaries may be impossible for your partner to keep because of his or her lifestyle or belief system. If the boundary is, "Do not eat sweets, bread, or anything fattening in my presence because I'm trying to lose fifteen pounds," it may be extremely difficult for your partner to comply. I had a client who felt that married couples should always go to bed at the same time and wanted his wife to hit the sheets at 11 P.M., when he did. The problem was, she was a night owl who didn't get tired until one in the morning. It wasn't a viable request—in fact, it violated *her* boundaries. In my opinion, it was reasonable for him to ask that she join him in bed at eleven for a half hour of cuddling so they could reconnect at the end of the day. After that, she would be free to leave. When you are committed to loving fearlessly, negotiating an outcome that will work for both of you becomes a top priority.

☀ Fearbuster Exercise: ☀ Can the Person Do It?

To determine whether your request can be met, ask yourself the following:

- Can my boundary-breaker realistically adhere to the boundary?

- Does this boundary take into account the lifestyle and needs of both of us?

- Does the boundary align with this person's belief system?

- Is it possible for this person to respect my request without constant reinforcement and support?

- Is this person open to negotiating or brainstorming ways to solve the underlying issue?

If the answer is no to one of the above, the boundary-breaker may not be willing or able to alter his or her behavior. In that case, you will be faced with a decision: Alter the boundary to be more workable for the other person, surrender to the situation and live with it as is, or walk away. It is your choice.

Step Four: Decide on the Consequences

If you are satisfied that your boundary is based on respect and is reasonable and viable, you must decide the actions you will take if your partner won't agree. *You do not need to share this information when you first request the boundary.* You want this to be a request, not a threat. I suggest that you make the request in a clear, compassionate manner, knowing in advance what you will do if it is denied or ignored.

The consequence could be as simple as no contact for a period of time or as serious as walking out the door. If, for example, your boyfriend refuses to stop teasing you in front of your boss, you may need to arrange things so that he no longer picks you up from work. Figure out how you'll get home without him before you have your discussion.

Step Five: Talk About Your Needs

Now the time has come to explain to your partner what you need and why. To be effective, a boundary must be clearly defined. Don't say, "I was wondering, would you mind if I left the room when you start yelling at me? I mean, if you don't want me to, it's okay. . . ." Instead, calmly and firmly state your truth: "I am no longer willing to stay in the same room with you while you are yelling at me. From now on, I will leave the room for ten minutes when that happens."

The same goes for longstanding agreements you wish to change. Don't ask, "Is it okay with you if maybe I quit going to your mother's every Sunday for dinner?" Say, "I no longer feel comfortable spending time with your mother every Sunday. I wanted to let you know now, so that we could either tell her together this Sunday or you can call and tell her yourself. I will commit to once a month." Your calm and friendly attitude signals that you have thought about what you're requesting and know that it's reasonable—not shameful, not selfish, not wrong.

When you are setting your boundary, make sure to explain why you feel the way you do. (If your mate has a tendency to use personal information against you, it may not be wise to share specifics. Rather, state your boundary and say something such as, "This is important to me. I would appreciate it if you respect it.")

If your partner is willing to honor your boundary, wonderful. You need go no further. If he refuses, explain the action you feel you need to take the next time your boundary is violated. Follow through. Take the action. Be a broken record, and continue to reeducate the person each time he breaks your boundaries, reminding him what the consequence will be and when it will occur.

Most people won't flatly refuse to honor a boundary. They'll agree to it and then forget or not take it seriously. The first time that happens, ask the boundary-breaker what he or she thinks an appropriate consequence would be. It's always better to invite them into the process than to make yourself the bad guy. For example, perhaps your spouse criticizes your cooking in front of your family. He realizes it's not respectful, but it's a habit he finds hard to break. Ask him to decide the consequence—maybe he'll get chivalrous and declare, "Every time I criticize the meal, you get a night out with your friends while I watch the kids." (Yes, that could happen.)

In some cases, the boundary-breaker will promise to comply but have no intention of doing so. He's just giving you lip service.

Let's say you're the night owl married to the husband who wants to go to bed at 11:00 P.M., and as soon as you start cuddling he can't bear to let you go. He uses every excuse, romantic and otherwise, to get you to stay. But you don't want to renegotiate. You don't want to go to bed early or make love. You want to finish cutting out the living room curtains so they will be ready for sewing tomorrow.

Firmly remind him that he is violating your boundary and that you plan on sticking to it tonight. If he refuses to listen, you might sleep in another room for the night. If he continually violates it, you may have to take more drastic measures. When things start escalating like that, it's wise to get support from a licensed therapist to help you fine-tune your stance. A mate who is that inflexible about a relatively small boundary is usually harboring deeper issues.

When someone continually ignores your boundaries but tells you he is trying to change, be careful. This person may be potentially abusive. You need to reinforce your boundaries and your worth by standing firm against any behavior that feels wrong to you, whether or not your mate acknowledges what he is doing.

The End of My Affair

In my own case, Eric would not discuss consequences because he didn't agree that he had violated my boundaries. I had to decide for myself what the consequences would be. I felt I could not simply leave him. I was afraid of what he might do to himself (he had threatened suicide) or to me (he was clearly unstable). I had gotten myself into a terrifying situation and had to work my way out boundary by boundary, watching every step, like a climber slowly rappelling down a cliff to the safety of firm ground.

The following words from Scott A. Johnson's *When "I Love You" Turns Violent* were what made me leave Eric once and for all: "Abuse is a choice." I didn't want to believe it, but I had to when I started to face what had been happening to me since he came into my life. Eric treated others differently than he treated me, which meant he had to decide to treat me badly. He had to make a choice. Eric wasn't at the whim of his emotions. He was in control of them and used them to manipulate me.

As I said before, knowing you have to leave and walking out the door can be miles apart. The first step was becoming aware. Next, I became very clear, calm, and conscious in every interaction with him. I didn't defend myself, I just restated the facts from my point of view. When Eric put down my friends, I would gently ask him to refrain from speaking about them that way. When he told me I was fat, I thanked him for sharing his thoughts and explained that it didn't help me lose weight. Could he instead work on helping me eat healthy meals when we were together? When he went on about how lucky I was to have him because I was getting old, I either ignored him or replied that I was only getting better with age. Each time Eric accused me, I answered him as lovingly and as firmly as I could. I had to be vigilant in my tone and language, because he was a master at twisting my words and using them against me. I knew that as I began to put boundaries in place, the truth would become evident. If I refused to accept Eric's version of reality and put more faith in my own, I would find out if he actually did love me.

It turned out he did not. The less effect his abuse had on me, the more abusive he became. He would force me to listen to him for hours as he berated me for being wrong, evil, or just plain stupid. "I'm only trying to help you!" he would shout. When I did not yell back and instead sat there patiently, it became obvious that my love made no difference. As he raged, I knew it wasn't about me. Eric was in his own world.

I think I had unconsciously believed that if I could change Eric I could have changed my father. It would have proved, somehow, that my mother didn't try hard enough. Setting boundaries and using them to evaluate what was really going on gave me the information I needed to see clearly. Eric was abusing me. It was my dad all over again. I had to get away from him in order to move on with my life.

It all came to a climax a couple of weeks after I began setting boundaries. We were at lunch and he accused me of flirting with the waiter. I had done no such thing and told him so. He backpedaled and joked about how the waiter was really hitting on *me*. "I didn't get that impression," I said. Feeling backed into a corner, Eric went storming up to the manager and demanded an apology from our waiter. I cringed. When he returned to the table, he had a huge grin on his face that seemed to shout, "I win."

For the rest of the meal, I only spoke when necessary. I didn't point out what he did. I didn't get disgusted. I didn't act cold. I didn't try to reason with him. I had finally reached my limit.

Eric knew the jig was up. He tried to joke in the car on the way back to my house, but I didn't joke back. I looked straight ahead. As he dropped me off, he didn't try to kiss me or come inside. His last words to me were, "I love you."

I walked into my house without looking back, and I haven't looked back since. I had cut the cord! I was free. Eric and I have not spoken or seen each other since that day.

The emotionally abusive relationship I had with Eric taught me many things. First, I learned to honor my essential nature. When I said no, I had to mean no. I promised myself that I would never again ignore my intuition. Regardless of how smart, confident, or healthy I appeared to be, this experience taught me that I was still susceptible to abuse. I also realized that if I had set boundaries at the beginning of the relationship, Eric's behavior would have surfaced sooner, prompting me to leave without investing so many months of my life.

Most important, I learned to trust myself before I trusted anyone else. Does this mean I will always be right about relationships? No. But if I follow the path of Fearless Loving, I will know what my boundaries are and when someone is violating them. I will know what my needs are and how to get them met by a man whose love is a match for mine. So will you.

Truth 7

Loss Is a Fact of Love

D-Day, 1998. On the anniversary of my parents' death, my divorce papers arrived in the mail. The irony was not lost on me. I was about to lose someone else I had thought would love me forever. As I read the words "no-fault divorce," I knew there was no such thing. Carl and I were both at fault, and we both would have to face our feelings of loss.

The loss of my marriage could have easily become a badge of honor, that is, proof of how much I had suffered and an excuse for not taking responsibility for my life. My parents' death had been a badge of honor. Their tragedy had hung over me for years, running every part of my life and influencing every decision. Back in my fear-filled days, I thought my attachment to my parents proved how much I loved them. Was I going to do the same thing with Carl? Was I willing to spend the rest of my life miserable so I could tell myself that he hurt me and I was wronged?

Several years earlier I had done the inconceivable. I had faced the loss of my parents and forgiven them. Not only had I survived, I had thrived. Now it was time to do it again. It was time to face the loss of my marriage, the loss of my dream of forever after. The loss of the hope that Carl and I would work it out no matter what. The loss of being left.

Because of my parents' death, I knew that even the most profound losses can be lived through. Not forgotten, but forgiven. Not resolved, but released. And our losses must be faced if we are to claim the love that is rightfully ours. For there is no love without loss. Loss is part of every human relationship; there is no protection against it or way to escape it. Our ability to embrace, process, and move through loss is a sign of how willing we are to truly love.

When my parents died, I began a lifelong quest to make sense of the loss I had suffered at such a young age. I studied philosophy and religion, trying to come to terms with it. The great teachers claimed that loss did not exist on a spiritual plane because we cannot lose what we do not own. In theory, I absolutely agreed. It just didn't feel that way when my heart was broken, or a dream was dying, or my husband was walking out the door.

Regardless of our path, loss is at the center of how we make decisions. We avoid love so we won't get hurt. We refuse opportunities so we won't have to risk losing face, money, position, or pride. We cling to our losses, wearing them as our badges of honor and using them as evidence that we shouldn't love because we will only lose again. But we are going to lose anyway. Denying love doesn't protect us from loss, it just makes us smaller, weaker, and more fearful.

So how do we embrace loss? How do we go on living in a hopeful state when loss could be right around the corner? I had begun to answer those questions when I forgave my parents, and as I stared down at the divorce papers, I knew I had still more to learn about loss and love.

What You Lose If You Don't Dare to Love

We live knowing we will die. We love knowing we will lose. Still, love is the only thing worth living for. Our love for our parents, children, friends, family, and pets keeps us plugged into life. A person who is serious about avoiding loss would have to reject her parents, refuse to have children, keep everyone at arm's length, and give away her pets. I've never met anyone who consciously wants to do this. Yet I have met people who claim to have sworn off love: "No more heartbreak for me. I'm perfectly fine alone, and I have no intention of getting hurt again."

Now, I'm a big advocate of loving yourself and living your life fully, whether or not you have a partner at the moment. But to reject the possibility of falling in love? To *intend* not to love because you expect to get hurt? To avoid connection in order to avoid pain? Not me.

I, like you, have lost many things. I lost my parents at the age of fourteen. I lost my love of God at that same moment, only to painfully recapture it many years later. During my marriage, when my husband and I learned we were unable to conceive, I lost my dream of being a mother. When I got divorced I lost the hope of a successful marriage and the security of being a wife. When I fell in love with Eric and allowed him to abuse me, I lost the image of myself as an evolved, perceptive, smarter-than-average gal. Every one of those losses was extremely painful, yet they were also freeing. They showed me how to love more deeply, more completely, and with fewer expectations. The life I have now and the woman I am today is mostly due to my losses and the way I moved through them. And in spite of what I have lost, I am ready, willing, eager, and able to love again.

As a coach, I have seen what people lose when they are too

185

afraid to love. Even if they don't come out and tell me they will never fall in love again, I can read it in their words and actions. These are the people who won't date until they are "ready"; who set absurdly high standards for potential mates; whose lives are so rigidly scheduled that they can't fit anyone in; who have been betrayed or rejected and can't get past the pain; who don't trust themselves not to make the same mistakes over and over again; who believe that if they can control their life they won't have to experience loss.

These men and women live by expectations rather than intention. Most of their waking hours are spent in "protect" mode, as they nervously wait for someone to cross a boundary, disappoint them, leave them, or not love them enough. They expect their loved ones to be predictable, their job to be the "same ol' same ol'," and the people they know to remain unchangeable. When you live with expectations like these, you suffer great loss even if you don't realize it. You lose new opportunities. You lose a sense of wonder and anticipation. You lose potential relationships. You lose peace of mind. You lose trust in yourself. You lose hope. You lose faith in other people. You lose optimism for the future. In the void that is left from those losses, fear leaks in—fear of being alone, unloved, disconnected, and dead inside. In trying to avoid loss, you lose more than you ever would by accepting it as a fact of life and moving through it.

The work you did in Truth 1, when you mapped out your Love Legacy, gives you an idea of how much your current attitude about love may be coming from a fear of loss. Perhaps you are afraid to reach out to another because no one ever dried your tears or loved you unconditionally. Or maybe every relationship you have been in left you with a broken heart. We all fear losing love; it is only natural. Our challenge is to recognize when our fears are so overwhelming that they are preventing us from loving again.

The Only Way Out Is Through Forgiveness

Of all the losses that bring people to my workshops, loss of a relationship has to rank number one. It is easily the biggest obstacle to falling in love again. Once burned, twice shy. Three or four times burned, and you're overscheduling your days like crazy and developing an emotional suit of armor. Fear sets in, bringing out the worst in you and making you forget that you are essentially a loving person. It is particularly bad if you were the one who got left. Rejection stinks, even if your mate didn't deserve you, mistreated you, and was all wrong for you. It hurts even if your friends thought he was creepy and your mother had bad dreams about him. In fact, if other people warned you against him (or her), it only makes the loss worse: you've been rejected by a person you were a fool to love in the first place, and everyone could see it but you. Anger, self-loathing, sadness, and fear can start to pull you under, making new love unimaginable. Forgiveness is the life raft that will bring you back to shore.

Yes, forgiveness. The very last thing you want to do. The thing that feels totally beyond your strength. You need to forgive the one who broke your heart, and then you need forgive yourself. You will do it for you, not for the other person. You will do it because the only way out of the pain of loss is to forgive and let go. I know firsthand, because forgiveness was the life raft that saved me from the undertow of my divorce.

The Showdown

I read over my divorce papers at the kitchen table, rage welling up inside me. All these months I had focused on being positive, empowering, and loving, but with the papers in hand my resolve drained away. Why hadn't Carl tried harder? Why wasn't I worth fighting for? Why did I stay so long in a marriage that was unfulfilling? I couldn't believe this was happening to me. As my anguish grew, I knew I needed more than pat psychological answers about why the marriage had come apart. What I really wanted was closure. I wanted to put this behind me so I could walk away with my soul intact.

When Carl stopped by later that afternoon to pick up his mail and a few more boxes, I was waiting. I had been so calm and considerate throughout the separation that the last thing he expected was anger. But that was all I had left. Anger at him for leaving. Anger at myself for letting him. Anger at his casual, carefree attitude about it all. I was through being Mrs. Nice Guy. I let him have it.

"Why are you over here? Didn't I tell you not to stop by without calling? Do you think I have nothing better to do than wait at home for you? Why don't you forward your mail like a grown-up? Why don't you leave for good? And quit looking at me like that. What is your problem, anyway?"

"What is *your* problem? Why are you so angry?"

"That's a dumb question. I'm angry because of you."

"What did I do?"

"Nothing. That's the problem. You did nothing to save our marriage. You did nothing you said you would do. You didn't try to win back my love. You won't tell me why you're leaving me. You won't tell me what went wrong. You won't even discuss our divorce."

"What do you want from me?" he replied, clearly annoyed at this inconvenience.

"So glad you asked," I said, my voice rising. "I want an apology. I want to hear you say, 'I'm sorry, Rhonda, for putting you through this. Sorry for lying to you for years. Sorry for being so la-de-dah about it all.' I want an apology for all the pain you've caused me. That's what I want."

He looked at me, shrugged his shoulders, and said, "Sorry." Then he walked out, still rifling through his mail as if nothing had happened.

Oh, I wanted to kill him at that moment, with his smug expression and his "I don't have to deal with you anymore" attitude. It burned a hole in my heart. Who was I kidding? He had never talked to me during our marriage, so why would he open up now? Carl himself probably didn't know why he left. How could I expect a sincere apology from a man who didn't have a clue what I was talking about?

And to think I had half expected him to fall on his knees and beg my forgiveness that day. I had secretly fantasized that when he saw me holding the divorce papers, he would stop in his tracks and realize what a fool he had been. I had said I wanted closure, but it wasn't true. I wanted him to come back. With that realization, I cried for the loss of my marriage like I never had before. Regardless of whether I acted loving or hostile, Carl was gone. I had to face the hard, cold truth before it froze my heart for good.

My Angel of Divorce

It was time to forgive. Forgive Carl, myself, and our marriage. It was time to heal, with or without his participation. This wasn't about him anymore, this was about me. As I contemplated what would help me forgive and let Carl go, I reflected on the ritual I had created for forgiving my parents, which I shared in *Fearless Living*. On that occasion, I had gone with Marta to a lake above Los Angeles and let the natural surroundings and solitude help me through the process. I didn't want peace and quiet this time, I wanted support and friends, a party as opposed to a sanctuary. That was it—I'd have a D-Party, short for Divorce.

I sat down and scribbled three requirements. It would have to be festive. It would have to help me face my loss and release it. It would have to be witnessed. You don't necessarily need witnesses for a healing ritual to be successful; the act itself is what heals. Some people prefer to be alone or with a single friend, as I had done with Marta at the lake. For others, a spiritual presence such as Jesus or Buddha is enough. This time, though, I knew I had to be surrounded by people who loved me. I wanted witnesses so that when all was said and done, they could remind me that I *did* do it. I *did* move on. I *did* forgive. They would remind me that the marriage was over and there was no going back.

I invited nine of my most loving, faithful, fearbusting friends and asked my spiritual mentor, Reverend Joan Steadman, to lead the celebration. Marta took charge of food, drinks, and creating the divorce cake. A gag cake wouldn't do. This was serious spiritual business, and I wanted the cake to express my true desire to recommit to partaking of the sweetness of life. The cake Marta brought was white inside and out to remind me that I was purifying myself when I took a bite. The filling had lots of fresh, plump berries, representing the abundance of the earth. Colorful frosting flowers adorned the top of the cake, a symbol of the love that is always blooming among friends.

I also wanted a lasting symbol of the D-Party, something that would remind me in the months ahead of what I released, forgave, and reclaimed. I found it on the floor of a furniture store covered with dust. It was a stone angel, antique white and covered with delicate cracks. It was perfect. At three feet tall it would stand as a monument, reminding me that I am blessed regardless of the appearance of my failed marriage. I took the angel home and kept it covered until the D-Party.

The week my divorce became final, my dearest friends and Reverend Joan arrived at my home to complete my marriage and celebrate my divorce. They brought food, drinks, and flowers. Some brought gifts. With sparkling punch in hand, Reverend Joan asked my nine witnesses to form a circle around me. As I stood in the midst of these powerful women, I felt lifted up by their love and strength.

Reverend Joan spoke of love, loss, and heartache. She talked of hope and faith. We wept, laughed, and reflected together on the seven years of marriage Carl and I had just completed. As she blessed my past, she nodded to Marta. It was time to bury my pain. To symbolize it, I had unwrapped my very dried-out wedding bouquet. (I keep everything.) Reverend Joan led us outside into the garden I had spent many hours creating, a fairy-tale oasis spilling over with flowers. Today it was more than a garden, it was a burial ground. I picked a spot near my favorite rose bush and began to dig. My friends joined in. We dug with spoons, not too deep but deep enough to place my dried wedding bouquet in the ground. As I took the bouquet from Marta, I lit a match. I knew I had to burn it or the burial would not be complete.

All those years in storage had turned the flowers into kindling. Within seconds the bouquet was a blazing torch. I could barely stand to watch my love literally going up in smoke. Tears were streaming down my face, and I sat down on the ground and began to wail. My witnesses took turns rubbing my back as my sobs became uncontrollable. I was beside myself. This was not the closure I thought I would have, but it was the release I needed.

I placed the burned stump of the bouquet in the hole with the rest of the ashes and furiously began covering them with soft earth. I didn't want to see a speck, a dust, an ounce of it. I knew if the bouquet was buried, I was in some way letting go of Carl. As I patted down the soil, I began to repeat, "I am willing to forgive Carl. I am willing to forgive myself. I let go of Carl. I let go of our marriage. I let go." Over and over, until my wedding bouquet was a mere pile of dirt under the shadow of my True Love roses.

With the flowers in the ground and my tears under control, Reverend Joan led us all back into the house, and my friends again formed a circle of love around me. This time Reverend Joan asked each of them to give me a gift, a quality they would like me to have for the next phase of my life. One by one they named their quality and the reason behind it, and once again, I wept. Victoria gave me courage to love again. Kim gave me joy so that I would always have an open heart. Lisa gave me trust. With each quality, I felt as if my friends were putting me back together piece by piece. I was starting to feel alive, more like myself, in fact better than the self I had known before.

When everyone had named a gift, Marta lifted the angel onto the table. I asked each person to speak their quality out loud while simultaneously touching the angel. This, I believed, would somehow imbue the angel with their gifts, so I could gain strength from them any time I looked at the angel, my angel, the ultimate D-Party witness.

When the last of my friends hugged me good-bye that day, I knew I was going to be all right. I had released. I had forgiven. With their help, I had reclaimed the parts of myself I thought had been lost with my marriage. I felt whole once again.

In the years that have passed since that incredible day, I have learned that forgiveness is not black and white. It is not a one-time event. Forgiveness happens in layers, like peeling an onion. The first layer is very challenging to get through. The skin is tough, and can be difficult to break open. The divorce party was my first layer, and it was the one of the hardest things I have ever done. But once you get past that layer, the skin sheds quickly, and you begin to see the vast treasure of new freedoms you can enjoy now that you are no longer bound by loss.

It works the same way no matter whose loss you need to release: a friend, a child, your parents, or the man or woman you love. It works whether the person deserted you, betrayed you, died, or simply moved on. I am not saying it is easy, or that it works all at once, but forgiving and letting go is the only way I know to move past loss and into freedom and hope.

Today, I can honestly say that I have forgiven Carl. He is remarried to a woman I have never met, and that is okay. I wish him all the best. He is not mine any longer. In fact, he never was.

Forgive Yourself, Too

When you forgive, you do it not for the other person but for yourself. The act of forgiveness allows you to make peace with the people or situation that has been tormenting you. It comes down to a willingness to get over what you think should have happened and accept the reality of the present moment.

Sometimes it is not enough to forgive the other person. Sometimes you are not only hurt by their behavior but also disgusted with yourself. As if the loss of the relationship weren't bad enough, you may absorb the other person's reasons for rejecting or mistreating you. You may have to keep reminding yourself that whatever they felt about you, it was not the whole picture. Even worse, you may feel intense disappointment in yourself, as I did in the breakup with Carl. If it wasn't a no-fault divorce but a both-fault divorce, maybe I should have been more patient, attentive, loving . . .

The Fearless Loving Truths brought me out of my despair. Even in the midst of my self-doubts, I knew that in order to recover from the loss of what had once seemed like a great love, I had to forgive not only Carl but also myself.

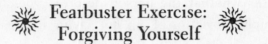

Fearbuster Exercise: Forgiving Yourself

We have so many seemingly valid reasons to continue punishing ourselves for our past that sometimes it seems hard to even think about forgiveness. Yet forgive we must. Without the healing power of forgiveness, you will be destined to keep repeating the same relationship problems over and over again. Answer the following questions:

- What beliefs or qualities are you fighting for that no longer serve you?

- What are your hidden resentments?

- What have you given up in order to be loved?

- What are you afraid will happen if you forgive yourself?

- What thoughts, words, and deeds are you ashamed of?

- What is the most devastating thing the world could know about you?

- What have you done in the past about which you still harbor regret?

- If you could change one thing about yourself, what would it be?

Each answer uncovers qualities or behaviors you would rather forget, parts of yourself that you do not accept. Forgiveness allows us to claim all of those lost pieces of ourselves. We feel whole again. We begin to accept ourselves regardless of our past actions or those qualities we think are intrinsic within us that cannot be changed. And the most wonderful result of owning yourself completely is that love has room to breathe. No longer are you worried about hiding or covering up or putting yourself down. You have more space in your heart for love.

After you answer each question, I want you to use those same answers and fill in the blank, one answer per blank. Repeat the phrase as often as necessary.

I am willing to forgive myself for————————————————————.

I am willing to forgive myself for————————————————————.

I am willing to forgive myself for————————————————————.

Saying you forgive may feel like a lie at first. That is normal. We have usually harbored these feelings for a long time and have built up good evidence to justify keeping them in place. That is why I included the powerful word *willing*. Willingness is the difference between staying stuck and being free. You just have to be willing.

It may sound simple but I guarantee that is all you need to begin to see profound change. Being willing will begin to heal your heart, giving you the courage to once again believe you can love fearlessly.

Not Closure, but Closer: Jerry's Story

When a marriage ends, you are losing much more than a partner. You are losing your image of yourself as a wife or husband, your dreams of the future, security, social standing, perhaps the possibility of having children. It is a tremendous loss, but you do have some control over how much pain it causes you. You can choose to forgive and let go.

Jerry and Katrina married right after grad school, to the delight of both their families. It was Jerry who urged Katrina to marry him, and Jerry's family who hosted the Fourth of July wedding at their large suburban home. They were in love, but just as important, Jerry felt that he and Katrina were an ideal match. She was an engineer, he a computer programmer. They each landed a well-paying job after graduation, and Jerry assumed they were on their way to a happy and predictable future.

Instead, fifteen years and two kids later they fought constantly, sometimes head-on and sometimes through silent punishment. The only reason they stayed together ate breakfast with them each morning—their two sons were the light of their lives. They had talked about splitting up but knew how hard it would be on the children, and they didn't have the income to do it anyway. Divorce was not an option.

Every once in a while, Jerry and Katrina would have some fun and forget about their ongoing conflicts, but it only lasted a day or two. It was right after a relatively calm weekend that the unexpected happened. Katrina woke Jerry in the middle of the night and told him her head hurt badly, that he had to call an ambulance. Three days later she was pronounced dead, the victim of a stroke.

For months afterward, Jerry felt deep sadness, loneliness, and shame. He tried to be strong for the boys, but felt guilty for any moment of happiness or peace.

"It wasn't an easy relationship, but I keep reliving our last few days together and thinking I should have loved her more. And I hate myself for admitting it, but my life is a lot easier now that she's gone. It's a huge relief not to always be fighting with her. I feel like I'm down to three emotions—guilt, relief, and sadness. Why did this have to happen to us, to the kids?"

My heart went out to him. "Most of us have an inner need to know the 'why' of a situation, yet the 'why' is usually what keeps us swirling around in the problem. It keeps the situation stuck in our mind, when what we actually need to do is let go with our heart. My parents died when I was fourteen. Will I ever fully understand why? No. Did I have an opportunity for closure? No. But have I healed and moved on? Yes!"

I went on to tell Jerry about my forgiveness D-Party, and I sketched out a similar plan for him. I wanted him to focus on moving through his loss and finding peace within himself. He had done the best he could with the information and experience he had. Feeling guilty and ashamed would not help him love his children better or open his heart to more love. I urged him to do one ceremony with his friends, and a week or so later, another one with his children. Together they could help one another find ways to continue to love Katrina and let go of their guilt for still being alive.

If you have been stuck trying to understand why a relationship didn't work, or are unwilling to forgive yourself, or are having a hard time letting go of a loved one who passed on, this will help you move forward and release the loss from your heart.

Fearbuster Exercise: Healing the Loss of a Relationship

- Write a letter to the person who has hurt you, left you, or betrayed you. Write as quickly as you can. Do not think about what you are writing. Let all of your feelings come up. Spill everything onto the page. When you are done, put it in a safe place where no one can find it. Now, do it again. And again. And again. Write until there is nothing left to say, positive or negative. Write until you feel like a broken record. Now, take all of your letters, bundle them together, and burn them. If that is impractical, tearing them up in tiny, tiny bits will have the same effect. As you burn or rip them up, you might want to say a blessing to send them on their way, such as, "I am grateful for all I have learned. I am grateful for all this relationship has given me. I am grateful for who I am becoming. I let go of our attachment. I release everything with love. I am willing to see the love."

- Write a reply letter to yourself, as if the person you lost were writing it. Write all the things you wished he or she would say. Carl never said he was sorry or showed any regret. It hurt. I wrote a letter to myself saying how sorry he was and how he wished he had worked harder on the marriage. Don't hesitate to write everything you have ever wished to hear. It's okay. Go for it. Then read it daily until you no longer feel angry, resentful, or bitter. Read it until you believe it.

- List one hundred acknowledgments about yourself including the lessons you learned and the skills you mastered due to this relationship. If one hundred is overwhelming, start with ten and keep going. Write each statement as follows:

  I acknowledge myself for ————————————————.

- List one hundred things you are grateful for about this person and this relationship. If one hundred seems impossible, start with ten and move on from there. Fill in the blank:

  I am grateful for————————————————————.

- Practice willingness. Practice forgiveness. Fill in the blanks. Repeat as often as necessary.

  I am willing to forgive ————— for ————————————.

  I am willing to forgive myself for ————————————.

This Fearbuster Exercise is about helping you move through the pain, honor the gift of the relationship, and forgive. You may have to go through the process more than once before you begin to get a sense of peace, because healing from the loss of a relationship is not a one-time event. I myself wrote several letters after my divorce. Writing the letters and burning them is especially therapeutic when you aren't sure what has gone wrong or what motivated the other person to leave. Rather than spending months or years trying to figure out why, begin to heal yourself now. Let go of "why," "what if," and "if only." Think of letting go as a cleansing process that will prepare you to have more love in your life. Visualize that each time you get past the "why," you are healing your heart. And your heart is where love resides. Keep on processing, and you will learn how to move from your head to your heart. (And if you want more information about letting go, read Chapter 7 of my first book, *Fearless Living*.)

Don't Skip the Sadness

Some couples who split up have no doubt at all why they are doing it. They've been through the arguments hundreds of times, they've tried counseling, they've stayed together until the kids are in college, and now it's over. They don't desire closure, they desire movement—away from the loss, the memories, and the sadness. But you can't necessarily rush through loss.

Donna came to see me about four months after she and Will, her husband of twenty-six years, had divorced. Money was not a problem. Will had made a good living as a dentist, and Donna held a part-time position as a fund-raiser for a literacy program. She kept the family house, while Will moved several states away to begin life over in a smaller town. It was all very civil, very amicable.

"So why do I feel so sad?" Donna asked me. "I know Will and I made the right decision. The marriage felt bone-dead. We're still friends, and we always will be because of the children. I have no regrets, and yet for the past few weeks I've felt myself slipping into depression. I need you to help me get out of it. I want this sadness behind me so I can get on with my life."

"What's wrong with feeling sad?"

"I don't feel motivated or inspired. I thought that after he moved out I'd feel liberated, and for about a month I did. But now I'm starting to lose steam, and I don't like it."

Sadness is a basic human emotion we feel whenever we experience loss. It doesn't have to be a serious loss, such as the end of a marriage. It could be a loss you welcome, such as the loss of familiar surroundings when you graduate college, or the loss of the old neighborhood when you move into a new one. It could be the loss of the life you leave behind as you achieve more success. However, most of us lump sadness, regrets, and mistakes into the same category. If we feel sad about a choice we've made, we assume it's because it was the wrong choice. Fearing we've blown it, we deny the sadness and push ahead, never entirely certain we're on the right path. Or we stall out, afraid to go either forward or backward.

Fear tells you not to admit when you are feeling sad, even to yourself. Fear wants you to brush it aside, to pretend it doesn't exist. But when you deny the feelings moving through you, you may actually be keeping the freedom you crave at arm's length. The energy you spend distracting yourself from feeling sad is energy you could be spending somewhere else, if you would allow yourself to move through the sadness.

As I mentioned earlier in this book, I was raised in a community where expressing one's feelings was frowned upon. I consider myself an expert at both squashing my feelings, which is what I did most of my life, and naming and expressing them. I would never suggest that you wallow in sadness, only that you acknowledge it. When my heart is heavy, I have learned to allow myself to indulge in it a little. (Key word: *little*.) I give myself a day or a weekend and go for it.

One Saturday a few years back, after I had sold my house and moved into temporary lodgings, I drove out to the beach specifically to allow myself to be sad. Period. For two hours I sat wrapped in a quilt my grandmother had made me and did absolutely nothing. I didn't read. I didn't write. I didn't listen to music. I barely thought. I just watched the waves and felt the sand in my toes. I shut my eyes and lay back, feeling the ocean breezes rush over my body, and I imagined those breezes sweeping away everything that was not working in my life. Afterward, I walked barefoot to a nearby restaurant and sat alone facing the ocean, feeling more spirited than I had a few hours earlier. When I was willing to face my feelings of sadness, I was able to put myself back on the path to freedom.

"Sadness usually arises to let you know you're ready to let go of something," I told Donna. "Why don't you stop fighting it and just go with it for a few days? See what happens."

Donna called me a week later to thank me for giving her the internal permission she needed to feel sad. She discovered she had been pushing aside a feeling of loss for her family as a whole, rather than the loss of her marriage. Even though her children were grown, she felt guilty for not being a good role model: "They'll never get to toast me and Will on our golden anniversary." And despite her desire for freedom, she couldn't help feeling lonely. "Memories of the five of us together, when the children were young, keep floating to the surface. How do I get used to being alone and keep the past in the past?"

As humans we long to connect, and when our relationships change, aspects of our connections change. That is why Donna felt sad and swamped by memories even though she had wanted the divorce. I suggested that she redefine her relationship with her children as a first step in her new, more independent life. What opportunities were available to her now? Could she plan special get-togethers? Have more interesting, adult-style conversations with them? It was true that she and Will would not be role models for staying happily married fifty years. Could she perhaps be a different type of role model, one of strength, love, and adaptability? Or she might prefer to drop the role model concept altogether and allow her children to see her as a human being and friend. Whatever she chose, it was a wonderful chance for her to build a strong, solid, grown-up relationship with them.

"Loneliness is a yearning for more connection, so find new ways to connect," I said. "Talk to other divorced parents about their solutions. Become active in your community. Be willing to try new things. Ask an acquaintance to meet over coffee—maybe now that you have more time, you can become friends. Most important, connect with yourself. That connection will be a constant source of comfort in the years ahead."

Finally, I urged Donna to create a photo album filled with the memories she wanted to savor. "Throw out or give away the pictures that bring up painful memories. It will take you a day or two or maybe even longer to assemble the album. When you're done, put it away for a while. It may take time for you to start living in the present. That's okay. Be gentle with yourself. This is the time to practice loving yourself."

Donna's sadness would pass, but the freedom her loss made possible stretched out into the future. As she put together her photo album, Donna sensed that she was bringing closure to her marriage by honoring it as well as saying good-bye. The many hours she spent going through the photos gave her time to think about how her life could change. On her own, she no longer had to present a united front with Will but was free to say and do things that reflected her feelings and beliefs. She was free to love her children differently, expand her circle of friends, and experience life however she wanted. She was free to fall in love again. When Donna moved through her sadness, there was a new world waiting for her, all because she had had the courage to let go.

Betrayal: When Your Trust Is Broken Along with Your Heart

Samantha was in heaven. She had met Joshua five months earlier at a party, and from the moment they said hello it was as if they were speaking the same code. They seemed to share some inner understanding, to be bound together by a mutual bloodline or secret history. It was the kind of connection Samantha had heard about but never experienced.

And Josh was so caring. More often than not, when they got together he would bring her a small token of his love. It might be a flower from his garden, a bottle of her favorite wine, or a goofy card that expressed one of their many inside jokes. It really didn't matter to Samantha. Those things were just icing on the cake. What was most important was that at thirty-three she had finally met the man of her dreams. They talked about everything, even marriage. Samantha felt safe, cherished, and loved.

On the night of their five-month anniversary, Joshua didn't call at his usual time, 10 P.M. sharp. As this was a special occasion, she was worried. At 10:30, Samantha decided to page him. No reply. This definitely was not like Joshua. She paged him again and again, but still he didn't phone back. As the night turned into morning, Samantha became convinced something terrible had happened to him. At 6 A.M. a reply finally came, but it wasn't from Joshua. A woman named Christina called, demanding to know who had been paging her husband all night.

"There must be a mistake," Samantha said. "Unless I somehow got the wrong number. I've been paging Joshua Eakins."

"That's my husband. He's out of town on business, and he forgot his pager. Can I help you? Who is this?"

Without a word, Samantha hung up the phone. Oh yes, the

business trip. She vaguely remembered something about that. If he was on a business trip, this could be the same Joshua. And he had the same last name as her Joshua. And he had given her this pager number. Stunned, Samantha kept replaying the few facts over in her mind. Finally, many minutes later, she understood that it had to be true. She sat on the edge of her bed, still as stone, while the full force of it sank in. Joshua had lied to her for five months. He had betrayed her. He had used her, knowing full well that he had no intention of marrying her. He was already married.

How could this have happened? How could he have fooled her all this time? Was she an idiot? Samantha knew Joshua had an ex-wife, but he rarely talked about her. In fact, he never spoke at all about his previous life, claiming it was too painful. Sure it was painful—because there was no ex-wife. There was only a wife. A living, breathing wife who had been on the other end of the phone claiming that her Joshua and Samantha's Joshua were one and the same.

Five minutes later her phone rang. She looked at the number on her caller ID. It was Joshua. She let it ring and ring. Finally the phone was silent. He never called her again.

Samantha showed up at my door two months later, heartbroken, feeling foolish, and determined not to be betrayed again. In fact, she didn't ever want to love again. She just wanted to figure out how she had been deceived. What was wrong with her? Was she that stupid? Ignorant? Blinded by love?

"I always thought I was really smart about this relationship stuff. I never jumped in. I never lived with a man. I never took him to meet my mother before I was sure. But this time, I thought I *was* sure. I can't believe it. And the worst part about it is, he hasn't called to apologize or give me an excuse. Nothing. He just disappeared."

"Fear causes people to do things that are less than honorable," I said. "I know that doesn't make it any less painful."

"Less than honorable? He was a deceitful, lying snake. How can I ever trust anyone again? How can I trust myself, if I couldn't see through him?"

Those two questions were at the heart of Samantha's pain, as they are for anyone who has been betrayed. Betrayal comes in many sizes and forms, and I have seen too many of them. There are the office friendships that never develop into a sexual relationship but drain away one spouse's attention and devotion. There are one-night stands, serial lovers, long-term extramarital affairs, and the occasional full-blown bigamist who manages to keep two households going without either spouse knowing about the other. In the end, of course, the truth always comes out. Like all people who are betrayed, Samantha had been dealt a triple-whammy of loss: loss of the relationship, loss of her ability to trust men, and perhaps worst of all, loss of trust in her own judgment. At times, she felt as if she had lost her mind. She didn't just feel used, she felt stupid, ashamed, and disoriented. On top of it all, her heart was broken. And the one person she longed to run to for comfort was Josh, who had put her there in the first place.

Samantha was more fortunate than most. She wasn't married to Joshua and had no children with him. Still, she was badly shaken by the deception and felt deeply wounded. How could she trust again, when the loss she experienced didn't make sense to her? In Samantha's mind this should not have happened. And in a world without fear, it wouldn't have. But fear is behind many, if not most, of our relationships. No matter how ideal Joshua seemed, her fear of losing him had outweighed her common sense. Understanding how that happened would help Samantha regain trust in her own judgment.

I asked Samantha some basic questions I believe are predictors of someone's willingness to share his or her life with another. Did she ever meet Josh at his house? Did she socialize with his friends or family? Did he join her when she had a family get-together or office party? Did she have all his numbers: home, office, mobile phone, and so on?

"No. No. No. No. But he had a good reason for everything. He told me that because of his divorce he was forced to live at a friend's house. He felt uncomfortable about his living situation, so he preferred to stay at my place. His friend was funny about the telephone, so it would be easier if I just paged him when I wanted to get in touch. Of course, he called every night at ten, and he called me at work a lot, too." It had been so easy to accept his answers. They all seemed to make sense. She was in love. She had no reason to doubt him. Only in hindsight could she recognize how flimsy the answers were, and how odd his behavior.

Samantha will probably never know what motivated Joshua to lie about his marriage. Perhaps he was addicted to that feeling you get when you first fall in love. Maybe his marriage was in trouble and he really did love Samantha. It could be he was afraid of losing his looks or sex appeal. But whatever his reasons, Joshua betrayed himself before he ever betrayed Samantha.

"We betray one another because we are afraid of facing the truth about who we are, what we want, and our feelings about the life we have created. Instead we deny our choices, our feelings, our reality. We start lying to ourselves, and that makes it easier to lie to other people. The lies turn into betrayals, and take on a life of their own.

"You weren't stupid to love Joshua," I assured her. "You weren't crazy. If you felt loved by Joshua, his love for you was probably real on some level. And there is nothing wrong with wanting to hang on to love."

"I want to believe you, Rhonda. But how will I learn to trust men again? Or myself?"

"Trusting the opposite sex is always a risk, because love and risk are bound together. You don't get one without the other, and that would be true even if you had never met Joshua. You won't always be right about the men you choose. It's possible that someone might betray you again. If that happens, just remember, he isn't doing it to you. He is doing it to avoid his own fear, to hide from himself."

I put my arm around Samantha's shoulders and gave her a squeeze. "The most important thing is for you to trust yourself and accept yourself even if you aren't always right. Don't let Joshua steal your loving heart away. Don't let his fears determine your future. Don't let his inability to be true to himself stop you from being true to yourself. If you follow the Eight Truths of Fearless Loving, it will become easier to distinguish between the men who are honest and open and those who are letting fear run their lives."

Hearts don't necessarily mend overnight, but they do mend. When Samantha was willing to consider forgiving Joshua, she would know her heart was healing. When she forgave herself, it would be a sure sign she was ready to love again.

"In the meantime, what do I do with the hurt?" she asked. "I can't sleep at night. I'm obsessed with revenge."

That is when I assigned her the following Fearbuster Exercise. Although it feels like cold comfort at the time, the most wrenching experiences hold the most potential for learning about yourself, particularly your resilience and capacity for growth. This exercise helped Samantha focus on the gains that existed within her loss.

Fearbuster Exercise: Out of Darkness, Light

- List twenty-five things you learned about yourself in the relationship.

- List twenty-five things you can acknowledge yourself for, during the time you were in the relationship, and because of it.

- List twenty-five things you are grateful for in regard to the relationship.

- Name your intention for your next relationship. Commit now, while this relationship is still fresh in your mind.

Once you are able to acknowledge the past, you can begin to step into your future. No rationalizations or excuses allowed. Every relationship is a step into the unknown, and each time you are willing to open your heart, you are saying yes to love. This time it may not have worked out, but that isn't the point. Remember, in order to love fearlessly, you must be willing to practice being yourself. Whatever else happens as a result of this loss, you will certainly end up knowing more about yourself than you did before. Absorb the lessons, and don't let yourself off the hook. If you take responsibility for your part in the relationship, your sense of personal power will increase because you will be choosing to learn from the pain rather than merely blaming your partner. Instead of closing your heart, expand it. Above all, have compassion for yourself.

Losing the Soul Mate Fantasy

Loss doesn't always involve a person. Sometimes it involves a fantasy, but one so tantalizing that it becomes as powerful as a real human being. For many people, that fantasy is called a "soul mate."

Our expectations and past relationships make it hard to love fearlessly. Fearless Loving means explaining ourselves, being vulnerable, and taking risks. It's complicated, not to mention scary. What if we do all that work and the relationship fizzles? It's tempting to think, "Love shouldn't be this hard. It wouldn't be if I could just meet the right person, my soul mate. Then love would elevate me, not test me. My soul mate would see through my defenses and recognize my highest self. He wouldn't argue with me, because we'd be equals. I would never have to explain myself because he would understand me with a glance or a touch. And speaking of touch, the chemistry would be *hot*, and it would stay that way forever, and he would never gain weight or look old, except for a few attractive laugh lines."

No matter how mature you think you are, the image of a soul mate is hard to shake. That's how it was for Austin, forty-seven, who came to see me because he wanted to meet his soul mate. He told me he would accept nothing less.

"Are you currently dating?" I asked him.

"No, because I'm married."

"You're married, but you want to meet your soul mate." I could barely contain my chuckles.

"That's right. And I'm afraid my wife isn't that person."

"How long have you been married?"

"Eighteen years. And I'm closing in on fifty. This is my one and only life, and now I'm afraid I might have made a mistake."

I spent the next hour and a half asking Austin about his marriage. It seemed that nothing was terribly wrong, it just felt old and stale. He loved his wife, Rosa, but he loved her like a friend. The spark was gone. He thought their lives would have been different at this point, more exciting. Instead he felt crushed by responsibilities. And time was going by, he kept reminding me. Austin had midlife crisis stamped all over him, and Rosa was apparently going to take the fall for it.

Often when a man reaches forty or fifty, he begins to tally up his personal score. What should he have accomplished by now, and what has he actually done? If he finds himself lacking, the world starts to look very bleak. He remembers the plans that never materialized, the stocks he didn't buy, the promotions he didn't get, the chances he didn't take. His wife has been a witness to it all. She doesn't need to say a word; it is their shared history that causes her husband pain. When he looks at her, he sees his failures. He projects his loss of youth and lack of success onto her, and soon a solution begins to emerge: If he leaves her, he can leave his failures behind and start over. It's no secret that men often blame their unhappiness on a stale marriage when the real cause is their own fear of being inadequate or growing old. Austin seemed headed in that direction.

"Did I make the wrong choice with Rosa?" he wondered. "Could I do better? Is my soul mate out there somewhere?"

"Does Rosa think you're *her* soul mate?" I asked.

"I have no idea. Never thought about it." And then he was off again with his list of grievances: Rosa probably didn't care about soul mates because she was too practical, not the romantic type, more concerned about what's for dinner, too busy. Finally I held up my hand.

"Okay, I get it. Austin, rather than focusing on Rosa, I think you need to figure out exactly what your soul mate would be like." As a homework assignment, I told him to choose the top five qualities his soul mate would possess. He went away happy as a clam.

The following week Austin eagerly handed me his list of five qualities and said, "What's next?"

"I want you to spend the next week keeping track of all the ways Rosa demonstrates these traits."

His face dropped, and then he got angry. "What for?"

"Because I want you to be aware of what you have before you make the decision to lose it. You're at a crossroads, Austin, and you are going to lose something regardless of which road you take. Either you will lose your wife and family, or you will lose your fantasy soul mate. I want you to make that choice with your eyes wide open."

Midlife is a time of change for both men and women, and change always brings loss. A short list of possible midlife losses includes youth, looks, perfect health, great eyesight, parents, hair, and a flat stomach. There are tremendous gains at this time as well, including credibility, respect, interesting work, a higher standard of living, the warmth of decades-long friendships, and watching your children grow up. But the losses loom large, especially the loss of youth and youthful expectations. The challenge is to understand the loss you are feeling, name it, and accept it for what it is. You can't escape it, not even if you try to cheat by running away from your past as Austin wanted to do.

I was tough on Austin. In addition to keeping track of the ways in which Rosa was his soul mate, I told him to list five things a day for which he was grateful to her. I wanted him to shift his attention from what she lacked to what she had. I also dared him to evaluate the kind of soul mate he had been to his wife. In order to have a soul mate, you must be willing to cultivate the characteristics you crave.

Loss awakens love. It forces you to re-examine your life and think about what really matters. Austin was right, time was passing by. He was getting older, and that made every moment more valuable. If he could accept the loss of his youth and some of his expectations, he could move on to the next phase of his life. I hoped it would include his wife, because throughout all our sessions he could give me no real reason to leave. After eighteen years of marriage they understood each other without having to explain themselves. Rosa knew Austin and loved him for who he was. They had a camaraderie, a repertoire of inside jokes, an intimate knowledge of how each other ticked—all the goodies you want from a soul mate. The catch is, you only get those goodies after spending years with another person. They are the rewards of commitment. If Austin was willing to make a commitment to his marriage, perhaps he could free himself of his imaginary soul mate and focus on the one who had been standing next to him all along. If he went out of his way to be a soul mate to Rosa, there was an excellent chance they would both feel the heat for each other again.

Lose the Fantasy and Gain the Present

Whenever you choose love, you are also choosing loss. The way you experience that loss depends on your perception of how things *should* be. When people get married, they usually expect it to last, yet half the time it doesn't. People expect to live a long life, but sometimes they don't. These expectations are understandable; in fact they help make life bearable. But when your expectations are piled up so high that reality can't ever meet them, you are setting yourself up for heavy losses.

The men and women who want my help finding a partner usually walk in with an image of what love should be like and a long list of "must-haves." It's only human to fantasize, yet I am often amazed at the level of detail they use to describe their ideal mate. The current buzzword for this is *high standards*. "I want the best," these clients will tell me, apologetic yet cocky. "Don't I deserve it?" By *best* they usually mean, "exactly like me, only better—smarter, more interesting, wealthier, and more evolved." It's another version of the soul mate fantasy.

And then love strikes, and it is nothing like they imagined. Inside their happiness, they feel a great sadness. They think something is wrong with them, but there is nothing wrong. Feeling sad doesn't necessarily mean they made a mistake. They're just processing the loss of what they thought love should be and replacing it with the real thing. Some people can't reconcile the dream with reality, so they break off the relationship. They refuse to see the love in front of them because it doesn't match their image. But that image was not created out of love, it was created out of fear. Fear of true intimacy. Fear of being rejected. Fear of being inadequate. Whatever they were afraid they lacked—social standing, looks, intelligence, money, connections—was funneled into the image and labeled *high standards*. Real-life soul mates rarely meet the standard.

The people with high standards are often the same ones who are in a state of panic because they have missed a self-imposed deadline, such as getting married by twenty-eight or having two children by thirty-five. That sort of rigidity goes hand-in-hand with high standards. For every standard, they are narrowing their pool of possible mates and making happiness that much more elusive. Individuals with high standards end up keeping themselves so separated from the real world that there is very little room for love to grow. Maybe the combination that will make you happiest has nothing to do with being married by a particular age. Maybe your family will be completely different than anything you could imagine. Why should you limit life to what *you* can think up? Life has endless possibilities.

Married people also make the mistake of dwelling on their losses rather than moving through them. Like Austin, they become obsessed with the idea of where they think they should be. Maybe you made your spouse some promises when you first married and they have yet to come true. Maybe you fear they never will. Maybe you don't yet have the house, the dog, or the children. Maybe you are just barely keeping your head above water, and the thought of adding anything else weighs you down. And because you love your partner and want to make him happy, you try to accomplish the things you think he desires. But it is killing you. And you are afraid that you can't keep up, can't compete, and that it doesn't work. The fear, the loss, the sense of disappointment overwhelms you, so you keep beating yourself up and pushing yourself.

Face your loss. Face it, move through it, and go forward. Face the disapproval of your spouse. (Maybe he will understand. Maybe he feels the same way.) Face the challenge of reshaping your expectations into intentions. Let go of what you think life should be so you can experience the life you have. It may be hard to swallow, but this is it. Right now. This moment is the life you have created. You can change it, but first you must face your loss. When you do, your future can begin.

Loss is inherent in everything we do, even when life is steaming ahead and we are making great progress. I recall the first time I watched two trainers facilitate a Fearless Living Foundation Weekend without me. I had long dreamed of this moment, when the program I had worked so hard to develop could be taught by someone besides me. Yet a deep sense of loss moved through me as I watched them, because I realized I was no longer needed the way I had been before. Loss was the last thing I expected to feel that day, but feeling it didn't make me regret my choice. By that time, I knew that loss forces us to grow. It wakes us up. It creates a space within us so we can make the necessary changes that will alter our course in life. Loss is one way we are shaped into our greatness.

I know that my gravest loss, the death of my parents, propelled me to where I am today. It pushed me to uncover the fear hidden within me and share the process with others. From that tragedy, I learned that loss isn't about your heart breaking. Your heart breaks so it can stretch past its apparent limitations to receive more love. Loss breaks your heart wide open so it can grow, expand, and heal the past. Loss shows us how deeply we are able to love, and love gives us the strength to face any loss.

Truth 8

Love Is a Risk You Must Take

Which do you trust, fear or love? You can only serve one master. If you trust your fears more than love, your life will be less than what you desire. If you trust love, get ready to be amazed by the gifts life has in store. Step into the world of risk, uncertainty, surprises, losses, success, pain, passion, connection, and courage. Love is not a prudent slice of measured experience. Love is the whole messy enchilada. There is no hedging your bets. It is not safe. It is not predictable. Love lives in the unknown. Fear thrives on safety, and love thrives on risk.

If you are one of those people who believes romance is not in your stars or that you are incapable of love, let me tell you a secret: Your fears have been lying to you. No one is incapable of love. There is no big love tablet with your name crossed off it. You write the tablet—you can choose to change the way you think and feel about the world, to open your eyes to the love around you, to open your heart to the love within you. You need only put your faith in love.

Just Say, "I Am Willing"

There is absolutely no way around it. If you want love, you have to be willing to risk. The key word is *willing*. Willing to be open, to see people as innocent, to see yourself differently than you have before. Willingness is the attitude that will change your life.

Marianne Williamson, foremost expert on *A Course in Miracles*, was the first to show me the power of *willing*. During the most frightening moments in my life, when I cried like there was no tomorrow, when dying sounded good, I repeated a phrase I learned from the *Course*: "I am willing to see this differently." I am willing to see my mate differently. I am willing to see this situation differently. I am willing to see this relationship differently. I am willing to see myself differently. I didn't have to know how to do it, and I didn't have to succeed. I only had to be willing to try. Being willing takes the pressure off. It takes the "I must be perfect" excuse away. It takes away every reason to beat yourself up.

Willingness opens the door to the unknown. It invites help and guidance from God, Buddha, Jesus, the fates, or whatever *unknown* means to you. The unknown can come in and alter a situation in a moment's notice, if you are willing to let it. Let's say your car gets rear-ended. You are willing to choose freedom over fear, so instead of scowling at the other driver, you choose to see him as innocent. You smile, shrug your shoulders, and decide to be nice. You leave it open. Who knows who this person might be to you? Maybe his brother is your future husband.

Or your ex-wife calls. She can't take your daughter to dance class after all. Instead of fuming, you cancel your tennis game and pick up your little girl. On the way to class she tells you what she dreamed last night, and it's the funniest dream you ever heard. You arrive at class still chuckling, and your smile makes you approachable. By the end of the class, you've met a single mom who shares your passions for tennis and Thai food.

That is what being willing is all about. Open, not closed. Floating, not fighting. Alert, not suspicious. In the moment, not in your head. You can plan and prepare and figure everything out to the minute, yet the miracles of life, those split-second revelations and random acts of kindness, come from your willingness to live in the unknown. If you are willing, you can change your mind, see things differently, start again. And new beginnings are crucial to love.

Whether you are willing or not, you do live with risk every day. I don't know what is going to happen to me, no matter how much I plan. I don't know what I am going to say, regardless of how I memorize my speech. I don't know how another person will react, regardless of my preparation for every scenario. I don't know, and neither do you. It's all a risk. The only thing we bring to the table is our willingness and our perceptions.

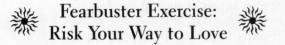

Fearbuster Exercise: Risk Your Way to Love

Answer the following questions. Do not filter. Do not think. Do not question what comes up for you.

1. What risks have you been avoiding in regard to __ love __ ?

2. Invent a way to take each of those risks.

3. What would you accomplish, contribute, or feel if you took those risks?

Most people know what they have been avoiding, they just don't want to admit it. But admitting it shows fear who's the boss. It breaks the hold fear has over you. Admitting the things you have been trying to avoid helps you take back your power. So go for it. If you need help inventing ways to risk, ask one of your Fearbuster Support Buddies to brainstorm with you to find a few ways you might move forward on each risk.

My clients use this exercise any time they feel stuck or overwhelmed about romance, or anything else for that matter. Fill in the blank with whatever is frustrating you. Here is how one woman answered the questions.

What risks have you been avoiding in regard to   <u>love</u>   *?*

Meeting new people.

Invent a way to take each of those risks.

Smile at three strangers a day.

Start small talk with one stranger a day.

Sign up for an Internet dating service.

Tell my friends to set me up with their friends.

What would you accomplish, contribute, or feel if you took that risk?

I would have no excuses not to date.

I would feel more desirable.

I would be taking responsibility for my love life.

I could potentially meet a wonderful guy.

Taking risks may be scary, but it is a requirement to being loving. If you are willing to love, you must be willing to risk.

Unknowable You

Expectations are the natural enemy of the unknown, and they are what most people use to control risk. Clinging to your expectations is like wearing blinders—you can only see what is directly in front of your nose. The rest of the world, the risky part you don't want to know about, stays outside your field of vision. It's all very familiar and safe. It can also be stifling, boring, frustrating, and depressing.

In order to remove your blinders, you first have to be aware that you are wearing them. The people who ask for my help finding romance are often saddled with three big expectations that blind them to love. They think they know all about themselves, they think they know their "type," and they think they know exactly the sort of relationship they want. Not true, three times.

Thinking you know yourself can be a great obstacle to love, because it sets up artificial boundaries. Maybe you don't have any children and aren't sure you would be a good mother. Does that mean all single or divorced dads are off limits? Maybe you view yourself as a nerdy, business-page type of guy. Does that mean you shouldn't ask the photographer down the hall out for a cup of coffee? No. None of us completely knows ourselves because we are always capable of growing and changing.

When we insist that we know exactly who we are, we are usually just listing our limitations and fears. How often have you said, "I'm not good at that," "He (or she) is way out of my league," or, "This is me. This is what you get." Each time you try to prove your limited view of yourself, you are being less than honest. You have an essential nature, a path that is available to you at all times, and if you deny it you are unwilling to experience your own greatness.

I used to think I wasn't funny or creative, two things I longed to be. For years, people would comment on my sense of humor or the unusual way my mind worked, but I thought they were crazy or just being kind. I was *not* creative. I couldn't draw a straight line, let alone paint a picture. And funny? Please. I was a very serious person, focused on serious things and living a thoughtful, serious life. I would argue with anyone who said differently, assuring them, "You don't really know me." What could people say to that? It ended every conversation.

Flash forward ten years. I now see that I am funny. Perhaps not the way a stand-up comic or sitcom character is funny, but funny. People who come to my workshops laugh a lot, and I love it. Creative? I created Fearless Living, which is enough to convince even me that I am a creative person. For most of my life I envied people with those qualities, only to discover in my thirties that I could rightfully claim both of them as my own.

What is beyond your reach? What do you think you can never do? Or be? Or have? How would your life be different if you possessed those qualities? What are you missing that you are convinced would put more love into your life? Repeat after me:

I am willing to see ———————————————differently.

Just be willing. Willingness signals your heart that it is safe to come out and play.

There Is No Such Thing as Your Type

The second misconception my clients get stuck on is their "type." They think they have one. Wrong again. There is no one type that will make you happy. You can be vigilant about following the Fearless Loving Truths, you can carefully choose your top five qualities, but none of that means the love of your life is going to show up looking like you imagined. When love arrives, the package doesn't matter because even though you swore you liked blue eyes, suddenly brown might seem awfully nice. You may think romance means gifts of flowers or jewelry until your new love gives you a bicycle, and all at once romance looks entirely different.

My friend Darlene called recently to tell me about her latest love adventures. She had done all the steps in Fearless Dating and was working hard to keep an open mind, regardless of her fears and expectations. The day she called, she was into the third month of a relationship with a man who was so far outside her box it scared her. She gave me the rundown.

"As you know, Rhonda, I have a bias against jocks. I figure they've got to be boring and probably sexist. I can't help it. I guess it's a leftover from high school. Anyway, Mark is definitely a jock. He watches sports on TV. He lifts weights. He skis. He plays soccer. He's in really good shape, but that sort of turned me off at first. It seemed like his muscles were bulging out of his clothes. He wasn't at all like the skinny, intellectual types I usually go for.

"The first date, I felt nothing. But your voice kept playing in my head: 'See his innocence, forget chemistry.' Date two, nothing. Date three, nothing. I had done what you requested, and could now move on to someone else. But then he called. I decided to chat with him rather than making an excuse to get off the phone, thinking it was a good opportunity to practice Fearless Loving. And then the weirdest thing happened. He made me laugh. It seems silly, but I didn't recall laughing on any of those three dates, and 'makes me laugh' is one of my top five qualities. When I laughed, I realized there might be more to Mark than met the eye. For one week we didn't get together at all, we just talked on the phone. I got to know him through our conversations, and on each call I laughed harder than the last time.

"Now we've been dating for three months, and I can't believe this, but the sexual chemistry is all there. When you first told me about your approach, I knew it had worked for your other clients but I thought, 'Not for me.' I was wrong."

The three dates in Fearless Dating are supposed to give you enough time to dig beneath first impressions, but if you typecast your date from the moment you lay eyes on him or her, your mission will be that much harder. Instead of focusing on whether or not the person is your type—physically, spiritually, politically, or otherwise—I challenge you to use the date as an opportunity to find out more about yourself and what you seek in a partner. Ask yourself: Do I enjoy his company? Does he have my top five traits? Is he kind? Compassionate? Good-hearted? Am I proud to be seen with him? Does he make me feel better about who I am? Can I speak freely with him? Does he care about my dreams and desires? Does he ask me questions? Do I feel more like myself in his company? Use the Love Log to help you see beyond types to the essential nature of the other person, and you may find out that your type is much different than you have assumed.

You Can't Balance Love

If it isn't self-defeating enough to think you already know exactly who you are and what your type is, some people also believe they know precisely how a relationship should be. They have it all mapped out. There is a code word they typically use for this plan: *balance.* If only they had a truly balanced relationship, they are sure they would have room for love, work, friendship, family, creativity, spirituality, and step classes. They just need to find the right formula and a partner who will go along with it. But how can life be balanced when you don't know what's going to happen next? Answer: It can't. Balance is an illusion. Balance is our desire to be in control of something that can't be controlled. Love is a risk. You must be willing to give up what you think has to happen in order for love to take root and survive.

Laura, a longtime client, told me she had decided how much time she could invest in a relationship. "I'm a career woman. If a man doesn't understand that, forget it. I work hard, but I lead a very balanced life. Yoga on Mondays, my Fearbuster group on Wednesdays, karate on Thursdays. Friday is girls' night out and with Sunday devoted to my family, Saturday is the only day I have to myself. It always seems I have to give up my life to fit a guy in. Not this time. I can date on Tuesdays. That's it."

Another client, Sam, confessed that he didn't see how he could balance his emotional life if he fell in love. "I have a daughter, and every time I think of how complicated it would be to add a woman to the picture, I just shut down. How could I balance my daughter and a serious girlfriend? Not to mention my ex. It would take a professional therapist to make them all happy."

Balance played out differently for Laura and Sam, but one thing they had in common was that when they said *balance*, they really meant *control*. The fact is, most of the elements in life that we wish to balance involve other people. In order to attain balance, we would have to control how much they need us and how much of our time they demand. There is nothing wrong with wanting to control yourself—to watch your feelings, think about your language, and be responsible for your actions and behavior. But you can't control other human beings.

Laura's plan to date only on Tuesdays was too restrictive—you can't factor love into a rigid schedule. Her balanced (controlled) week was really an insurance policy *against* falling in love. And Sam assumed he should be able to personally balance (control) the emotions of his daughter, a girlfriend, and his ex-wife. Although he would surely influence their emotions, he could never be entirely responsible for them. Did it make sense to resign himself to a life without love unless he could guarantee that everyone would be happy all the time?

Seeking balance, no matter how Zen-like it sounds, is sometimes just a cover-up for our desire to force love and life to unfold a certain way. If we are afraid the universe only has bad surprises in store, we set up elaborate schedules in order to control our experiences. If we are afraid we will fail or look foolish in new situations, we cling to familiar people and places—the rituals of a balanced day—so we can control the situations we find ourselves in.

When we first commit to someone, we often make agreements in the name of balance that bear no relation to the unknowns we will eventually face. Promises such as, "We will both pay exactly half the expenses," "I'll work and you'll raise the children," and, "We'll buy me a new car this year, and you a new car next year," inevitably give way to the reality that life is change. What happens if you get laid off? Or your career ends up leaving you frustrated and you want to start over? Or your husband decides to take a year off and write a novel? Are you going to complain that this wasn't part of the deal, or will you try to adjust to a lower income so he can fulfill his dream? And once children enter the picture, the unknowns multiply by about a thousand.

Clients often tell me they just want a relationship that is fair. Fair is a word of expectation, a word that implies we know better than anyone else what is right in a given situation. But what we believe is fair today may seem grossly unfair tomorrow. Just ask the husband who gets offered a job with a thirty percent pay raise but a two-hour commute, or the wife who decides she doesn't want children after all, or the mother who realizes she wants to quit her corporate job for a few years to raise her kids. In real life, love is rarely fair and equal. It is a long stroll into the unknown, taking risks each step of the way.

There is no deal you can make that will guarantee your relationship will be a success. There are too many twists and turns in the road ahead. Success can only be measured over many years, when a flow chart of ups and downs might reveal a pattern of support and commitment. Then again, how do you chart such things as getting up early to make your spouse breakfast, soothing each other's work worries, helping the children with their homework, and taking Sunday drives together? So many of the important things end up being impossible to measure. There will be times when one of you is absolutely wild in love while the other is concentrating on work. Then it will reverse. There may be months when you feel like brother and sister, and suddenly things will shift and you'll feel like teenagers again. It's unpredictable, untamable, and full of risks.

Love may be the one place where we wish that things would always stay the same so we could make rules and stick to them. But the person we want to love us the same way forever won't. It isn't possible. Love is not stagnant. It is not a one-time-only experience to be replayed over and over. We don't know where love will take us, what it will demand of us, or what riches it will lay at our feet. When we love, transformation, expansion, and growth are things we must encourage. When those occur, we learn to love from a place with more depth and more light. And it can only happen when we are willing to take chances.

Surrender to the Unknown

So you see, there is no way out. To love fully, you will have to surrender to the unknown. You will have to give up your preconceived notions about what you can and cannot do. You will have to forsake your "type" and look for the essential nature in every person you date. You will have to be aware when your desire for balance is really a desire to control others or avoid risk. You will have to surrender all your ideas of what love should be and have faith in the love that is.

Yes, it is tough to surrender. Who volunteers to jump out of a plane without a parachute? Sometimes that is what surrendering feels like. Surrendering is giving up your personal agenda, your need to obtain results in a specific way. Surrendering is letting go of what you think should happen so you can experience what is actually happening now. It is being willing to understand that you don't always know what is best for yourself. When you surrender to the unknown, you are allowing new and different possibilities into your life. You are admitting that there is a better way, and you don't yet know what it is.

Surrendering to my divorce was something I did not relish. Surrendering to loving again was something I resisted. Surrendering my home, and all that it meant, was not pleasant. Yet each time I surrendered, something better came along. It opened a world I didn't know existed. I learned to trust my instincts more. I grew in compassion. I expanded the definition of home. Each time I surrendered, I broke out of the confining box I didn't even know I was in.

Changing jobs, moving to a new city, or losing a relationship are things we all face as adults. Even if we welcome the change, there is always an element of fear and risk attached to something new.

Yet eventually we surrender to our new situation. Whether or not we wanted the change, we acclimate ourselves to it. Otherwise, resentment and frustration begin to brew within us, coloring our decisions. If that happens, fear has taken hold.

Surrender to the unknown. Surrender to being uncomfortable. Surrender to breaking your patterns once and for all. Surrender to doing the work necessary for real change to take place. Surrender to the very thing you know you want to do but are afraid to. Surrender to more love. Surrender to forgiveness. Surrender to the feelings moving through you.

Surrendering is not giving up. It is not compromising who you are. It is not turning your back on yourself. On the contrary, when you surrender, you actually become more of who you are meant to be. There is room in that "I don't know" space to move around, try things on, and practice new ways of thinking, speaking, listening, acting, and being. In that space, you have an opportunity to practice being you with a bigger heart.

Beyond the Comfort Zone

Surrendering to the unknown takes levels of courage you may not know you possess. This is called going beyond your comfort zone, and make no mistake, it can get very distressing out there. When you leave your comfort zone, your fears will show up, I guarantee it. Every instinct may tell you to run, hide, deny, and stay safe. Against that wall of fear you have only your commitment to love fearlessly. You know what that means: See people as innocent, stay true to your essential nature, and speak up.

Andrea had to step outside her comfort zone when her boyfriend's ex came into their lives. James had been madly in love with the ex, and he and Andrea had been together for only three months when she called. Andrea could hear James's voice change the minute he picked up the phone and realized it was *her*. After sidling into the bedroom for a twenty-minute conversation, he emerged red-faced and told Andrea that he and the ex had made plans to get together "just for dinner, no big deal." That's when Andrea came to see me.

"I don't feel comfortable about that dinner," she said.

"That's an understatement," I replied. "Who wants her boyfriend spending time with an ex he was crazy about? But that doesn't mean you should try to stop him. Consider the alternative. Do you always want to wonder if James loved his ex more than you? Or would you rather know the truth now?"

To me, the fearless path was obvious: Andrea could express her fears to James. He would then have to choose either to call off the dinner or go. If he decided to go, Andrea must honor his request without resentment, sulking, or pleading. Otherwise, James would feel controlled by her and their relationship would suffer for it. Andrea wasn't happy about this advice, but she agreed it was the most fearless and loving approach. When your commitment is to be loving regardless of the circumstances, there is no room for harsh words. You assert yourself not from a desire to control but from a desire to stand for who you are.

Andrea gathered up her courage and told James exactly how she felt about his dinner date. "I understand if you want to see how you feel about her. And yes, I'm scared you'll find out that you still love her, and then you'll leave me. But I also know this: I don't want a little bit of your love, the scraps left over from your ex. I want all of it. That's why I support your decision, whatever it is. And I know that by saying all of this to you, which is a first for me, I have learned to love myself a little bit more. Thank you for listening."

James did go on the date. He did fall in love with his ex all over again. Andrea was sad and hurt, but not devastated. She had chosen freedom over confinement. She had chosen to face her fears rather than run from them. She didn't date for a couple of months, choosing instead to give herself time to heal and process her feelings. Then, one morning, she knew she was ready to love again.

On her first date with Ed, he took her to the town's newest, most popular restaurant. Andrea felt good. She missed James but quickly reminded herself that she wanted big love, not little scraps. After the main course, she went to the restroom and on the way there ran smack-dab into James. He lit up when he saw her.

"Andrea! How are you doing? Man, have I missed you." He hugged her tightly.

"You have? Well, it's good to see you too, James. Gotta go."

"Wait. I was wondering if I could call you."

"What about your girlfriend? Are you still with her?"

"Yeah, but it's just about over. I think about you a lot. I want to see you again. I'm going to call you, okay?"

"No, James. Please don't call. I wish you the best." And with that she made her way to the bathroom. The first thing she did upon entering was brace herself against the sink. Her knees were weak and her throat was dry—James was every bit as hot as she remembered. He still made her swoon. Just the same, she started to smile. She had really done it. She had walked away because she knew James wasn't committed to the same kind of love she was. She had been true to herself and kind to James without giving in to him.

Andrea walked back to the table to greet Ed, knowing that love was expanding or contracting around her with every choice she made. She was willing to take a risk and discover who this Ed guy was. Andrea was going to be all right.

The Power of Yes

At the beginning of this book I said that loving is a verb. It is action and intention. It is a risk that we must take in order to find out who we are. The only part of love you can control is the part that comes from you, and everything else is the great unknown. Over the past few years, as I have embraced Fearless Loving as my path, I have committed to seeing the world through the eyes of love whether or not there is someone special in my life. I want to be in love every day, with everyone I meet. I want to feel complete with a man or without one. I want to be satisfied with my life even if I am not madly, deeply, passionately in love. I want to be happy with me. Just as I am. That is my goal. That is my commitment. That is my intention. That is how I make my decisions. That is how I find love, receive love, and express love—by freely giving of myself, knowing that there are no guarantees. I don't want guarantees. I choose to believe there are greater things in store for me than those I can imagine on my own. I don't want to know it all. When you know it all, love has little room to grow. When you plan it all, love has little room to perform miracles. When you want to be perfect, love has little room to heal, to enhance, to soothe you.

Each and every day, I randomly say thank you to God for the honor of being alive. I am determined to see the goodness in people even if they are not exhibiting it, because I would rather fall in love a hundred times than not at all. I would rather be overly generous than stingy. I would rather have faith than doubt. I would rather trust someone than question his motives. I would rather spend my time in peace than in anguish. I would rather be kind than careful. I would rather wake up happy to be alive than worry about what might go wrong. I would rather say yes than no.

In Truth 2, "Everyone Is Innocent," I told you that seeing people as innocent is fundamental to changing your relationships. You don't have to *believe* they are innocent, you just have to act as if they are. No guarantees. At first, this may feel like a colossal risk. When you finish reading *Fearless Loving* and start putting its truths into action, seeing people as innocent will be your biggest challenge. It is the one truth you will be refining, relearning, and rededicating yourself to for your entire life. And yet, if there is a Truth I could point to as being the most life-altering concept in this book, that would be the one. You can learn to follow the Fearless Dating plan, fill in your Love Log, stand up for yourself, process loss, understand boundaries, and honor your essential nature, but unless you are willing to see everyone as innocent, you will never float through life. You will always be swimming against the tide.

When you come down to it, seeing people as innocent is like saying yes to them before they ask for anything. It is an act of faith that comes from your highest self. There is a famous story about how Beatle John Lennon met the love of his life, Yoko Ono. An artist at the time, she had an installation set up in a gallery in New York City. One of the pieces consisted only of a ladder that reached to the ceiling. John climbed it, and in small type printed on the ceiling itself was just one word: *Yes.* John knew immediately that he had to meet the artist, and the rest is history.

I have seen the power of yes transform many people, but the one who stands out in my mind most vividly is Lisa. She was one of my very first clients and came to me specifically because she wanted to get married. In fact, she threw down a challenge: "Can you get me married within a year?" Feeling omnipotent that day, I agreed. At first things went amazingly well—within a month she had met a man who made her laugh, shared a lot of the same interests, and seemed as taken with Lisa as she was with him. She was ready to walk the streets with a sandwich board advertising my skills.

At the six-month mark, I received a phone call from her. "I'm halfway to the deadline," she joked. "I've found the guy, but he hasn't asked me to marry him yet."

"What do you do when he talks about the future?" I inquired.

"I don't know what to say. I just kind of look at him or maybe walk away."

"So when he talks about the future you give him a real clear "yes," don't you?" I teased her. "Most men need a yes before they ask. They have fears too, you know. The next time he mentions anything having to do with the future, say, 'Honey, that sounds really good,' and let him know that when you think about the future, he's always in it."

Lisa groaned. "Oh, God. What if he isn't hinting around after all?"

"So you think he's trying to trick you?"

"No."

"To lead you on?"

"No."

"So what's bothering you?"

Lisa laughed a little self-consciously and thought about the question. Then she confessed, "If a guy is really in love with you, he knows. And he's got the guts to ask you to marry him. That's the way I think it should be. Clear and strong, no ifs, buts, or maybes."

"But love isn't that neat. Love is messy. And if it isn't messy at the beginning of a relationship, trust me, it will get messy later on. If you feel sure about this man, let him know it. A year from now, you may be the one who needs to hear a yes. Go first! Take a risk. Give him a "yes" before he asks. If you start sending those "yes" signals, I think you'll know how he feels about you very soon."

Lisa's boyfriend did a lot of talking in the days that followed. He talked vaguely about next year; he talked casually about next Christmas; he talked theoretically about where the perfect vacation house would be. Each time he brought up the future, Lisa forced herself to join in by sharing her ideas or saying something as simple as, "That sounds nice," or, "I'd like that." He tested the waters no fewer than five times before he got up the courage to propose, exactly two weeks after Lisa started saying yes. She was married well within her one-year deadline.

When you assume people are innocent, you are saying yes to life and its possibilities. You are saying yes before there is proof, before anyone has earned it, before you know what the payoff will be. You are throwing open the doors, so that if love is out there, it will know it can come in.

Love or Fear: It Is Your Choice

So which do you trust, fear or love? Fear tells you to hide your true self. Love tells you stand up and shine. Fear wants perfection. Love is perfect despite appearances. Fear tells you being right is the way to stay safe. Love knows safety is an illusion. Fear argues for your limitations. Love takes a stand for your greatness. Fear wants more. Love knows there is always enough. Fear thinks pain is a weakness. Love sees pain as an opening. Fear wants guarantees. Love wouldn't ask for guarantees. Fear tells you to protect yourself. Love tells you to be vulnerable. Fear wants to know why. Love wants to know how. Fear wants to confine. Love wants to let go. Fear wants to hold on. Love wants to surrender. Fear wants to be wanted. Love knows it is. Fear judges. Love accepts. Fear tells you to sacrifice. Love tells you it's a gift.

What can you do to move out of fear and into love? You can begin by smiling at strangers or seeing your spouse as innocent. You can tell the people you work with that you are looking for love and ask if they know anyone interesting. Start small. Start somewhere. Just start. Love is not going to find you if you are hiding from the world inside your house, eating chocolate chip cookies and pretending it doesn't matter. It does matter. If you are reading this book, you want more love or deeper love. Pick one of the Fearbuster Exercises and begin to practice it so you can start loving fearlessly, one step at a time. And be prepared—your fears will not want you to listen to me. They will urge you to stay in your comfort zone, do the exercises later, and eat a few more cookies. They will tell you this is stupid or won't work or is not right for you. Do not listen.

As you expand your ability to take risks, fear will take a back seat to love. So risk. Risk being vulnerable. Risk falling in love first. Risk saying yes even if you are terrified the other person will turn away. Risk being you when your fears tell you to be anything but. Risk putting boundaries in place and saying no. Risk being worth someone's effort. Risk asking for love. Risk anything that stands between you and your ability to be the loving presence you are when fear is not running the show. Love may be rusty, but don't let that stop you. It's like riding a bike. Accept the risk. Get on and start pedaling. It will all come back—it always does.

Living with the
Fearless Loving Program

L ove gives us hope. Hope that life is good, that we are good, that the world is worth living in and fighting for. Love is how we get our number-one human need met, our desire to connect and belong. Fear, in an attempt to protect us from being hurt, stands between us and love. It keeps us distrustful, desperate, or jealous. Our intention may be to love, but fear overrides our essential nature, so we people-please, pick fights, become passive-aggressive, or give up. Fear makes love seem difficult or even unattainable. The Eight Truths in *Fearless Loving* are a pathway out of fear and into the love that exists both within us and around us.

How do you keep on the path? How do you stay committed to "being love" when love doesn't seem to be showing up fast enough or big enough? The secret is that love isn't about someone else loving you. It is about your ability to love yourself and the people around you, regardless of what the world does or doesn't give you. Fear wants you to measure how much love you are getting from the outside world as proof that this program works. But love isn't about outside proof. Love is an inside job. And in reality, *Fearless Loving* isn't about achieving a specific goal such as getting married, making your spouse treat you better, or finding a boyfriend. The heart of *Fearless Loving* is about changing your perception of yourself, and in so doing, altering the way you experience the world.

How will you know the program is working? When you realize that you are no longer as judgmental as you used to be. You aren't on autopilot, making excuses about your life and complaining about *those* people. You don't push love away like you once did, because you aren't afraid of getting hurt or being lied to. You trust yourself to recognize when others are reacting out of fear, and you know how to set boundaries if you need to. You realize that there is no love without risk, and you know you have the courage and the skills to handle it. The program is working when innocence, not fear, is your default position. When you give others the benefit of the doubt without thinking twice about it. When compassion comes easily. When you want to listen as well as be heard. When you improve your ability to stay focused on what matters most— your treatment of other people, not their treatment of you.

You will have truly learned the Eight Truths when you notice that the world is a kinder place than it once was. Trust has become second nature. Faith has become a way of life. The unknown has become a valued friend. No longer do you seek only the big love; you are attuned to the everyday love, the random moments of grace. You will have mastered the *Fearless Loving* program when you understand that the eyes you use to see the world determine the world you see, and all the love in your life springs from that vision.

Fearbuster Exercise: The Path of Fearless Love

I encourage you to list all the ways you are accepting love on a daily basis. Don't get caught up in the type of love you receive. For instance, don't dismiss the coworker who says, "I love you for that!" or an acquaintance who tells you, "I love your sense of humor." Accept it. List every type of love that comes into your life, including acknowledgments, compliments, and casual acts of kindness.

Next, list all the people in your life who love you. Notice if you have rules of love. Do you believe people love you only if they do certain things, have known you for long time, or have gone through a crisis with you? How many walls have you erected between you and love?

Finally, list all the people you love. Not just big love, but small love as well. Include your close friends from college even if you haven't spoken in a while. Include your child's best friend, if that friend makes your child happy. Who do you love? What is your criteria for loving others? Is there a moment that has to happen in order for you to love someone?

Knowing how you choose to love, and seeing how you keep love out, will help you focus on the Truths that are most important to you. I invite you to do this every few months to see how love is growing in your life. I know it works for me. For example, I used to feel guilty if someone volunteered to help me do just about anything—set up a stereo system, run an errand, tape a TV show. I thought I owed them. Now I see it as a gift of love. Instead of feeling obligated, I'm grateful for their love as well as their deed. As I embrace love in all the remarkable ways it shows up, I see more love everywhere. It is a gift I must be willing to accept if I want to grow in love each day.

I urge you to walk the path of Fearless Loving with an open heart and open mind. Don't give up. Just before the path gets easy there is always a steep hill to climb. It will feel like it is taking forever. It will feel like you'll never make it or things will never change. But I absolutely know that if you keep on loving using the Eight Truths as your guide, love will begin not only to look different, but also to feel different.

The *Fearless Loving* Truths are simple in principle, yet they may require you to make some tough changes. Fear will be a regular visitor when you are committed to practicing love on a daily basis. Remember, it is just an affirmation of your growth. Fear is trying to protect you from taking risks and stepping off the familiar path. When it shows up, thank it for caring, and start loving. Put the following Eight Truths in your wallet or on your wall, and allow them to remind you that this is what Fearless Love looks and feels like. Go on . . . "be" love.

The Eight Truths of *Fearless Loving*

Truth 1: Love Is Up to You
Love first. Love last. Love all ways.

Truth 2: Everyone Is Innocent
Fear is the only reason we judge someone else.
Accept the soul in front of you.

Truth 3: Feelings Lie
Honor your feelings. Act on your commitments.

Truth 4: Chemistry Is Between Your Ears
Sexual attraction lasts only when you let go of the fantasy
and embrace humanity.

Truth 5: Dating Is Where You Practice Being Yourself
Being you is essential in order to feel loved and "be love."

Truth 6: "Yes" Means Nothing If You Can't Say "No"
Boundaries tell you who you are, what you value,
and where you stand.

Truth 7: Loss Is a Fact of Love
Your ability to accept and move through loss frees you to
love.

Truth 8: Love Is a Risk You Must Take
Love lies in the unknown, and the pathway is risk.

The Wheels of Fear
and Freedom

The Fearless Living process begins by learning about and identifying what I call your Wheel of Fear and Wheel of Freedom. The Wheels represent two distinct modes of perception that influence our feelings and therefore, ultimately, our behavior. The Wheel of Fear acts as an unconscious system of defenses you use as protection from situations you believe will cause you pain. The Wheel of Freedom is an alternate pathway you use to change your perception of the world and free yourself from a fear-based perspective.

The Wheel of Fear

The Wheel of Fear is created by your family heritage, belief system, and life experiences. Everyone has a unique Wheel of Fear, but the mechanism works the same way for all of us.

There are four points on the Wheel. First, something happens that **triggers your fear** of being thought of by others as not being good enough. Neearly all of us believe we have a serious character flaw we must keep hidden from the rest of the world. Some people are afraid of being thought of as selfish. For others, it's being thought of as stupid, lazy, weak, ordinary, or phony. For me, it was being a loser. When an event occurs that threatens to expose this flaw, fear is triggered. Consciously or unconsciously, we respond by trying to avoid the threat. This sets the Wheel of Fear in motion.

Your **fear response** leads you to do something you believe will convince others that you do not have this character flaw. Let's say you're afraid of appearing selfish. A friend asks you to feed her cat and change the litter box while she is on vacation. You don't like cats and can't bear the smell of cat food, kitty litter, and most of all, what's *in* the kitty litter. But you are afraid of seeming selfish, so you agree.

Negative feelings are the next point on the Wheel of Fear. Now that you are caring for the cat, you feel resentful. You resent the cat and, worse, you resent your friend. Far from feeling magnanimous and helpful, you now feel more selfish than ever. The realization that you haven't avoided what you feared—being "selfish"—makes you even more disgusted with yourself. If you can't perform this small act of friendship without fuming over it, what good are you? What if a relative were sick? Would you rise to the occasion, or would that turn your stomach, too? Why are you so weak? Can't anyone count on you for anything? Truly, *you are not good enough.* And that is how the actions you take to avoid your "flaws" perpetuate them instead.

There is one final stop on the Wheel of Fear. You find a way to numb the emotional pain of facing your supposed flaw, usually some type of **self-destructive behavior.** Of course, anguishing over a litter box doesn't rate very high in the overall scheme of things, but pile enough of these small incidents on top of one another, and the self-hatred compounds. Larger events—at work or with loved ones—trigger more intense reactions in the Wheel. To numb our-selves, we turn to behaviors like overindulging in food, drink or drugs; shopping; sleeping with the wrong people; and isolating our-selves from family and friends. The self-destructive behavior brings you back to the beginning of the cycle. You have not dealt with your fear, you have only gone around the Wheel, and the next time you're faced with the threat of being exposed as "selfish" chances are you will react in exactly the same way.

THE WHEEL OF FEAR

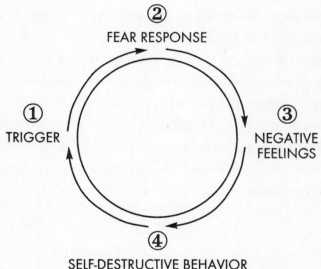

In *Fearless Living* I go into great detail about how to discover what triggers your Wheel of Fear. Here, I'll just mention that the trigger—be it selfishness, laziness, being a loser, or whatever—springs from a core negative feeling that you believe is true about yourself. Maybe you will recognize your core negative feeling the next time you wake up at 3:00 A.M. The self-loathing words you hear yourself thinking are usually spelling it out for you: "I will never be loved," "I am foolish," "I am insignificant," "I am damaged." We all have our own version of *I am not good enough,* and that is the core negative feeling our Wheel of Fear keeps trying to shield us from.

For example, if your Wheel of Fear is triggered by "selfish," your core negative feeling might be "I am a failure." For reasons unique to your own background and psychological makeup, you view selfish behavior as a sign of your failure as a human being. The Wheel of Fear exists to protect you from ever experiencing "I am a failure," so when presented with a situation where you think you might be perceived as selfish, the Wheel starts turning. Its goal is to make sure that others do not see you as selfish, so that you will not have to feel like a failure.

The fear trigger is to the core negative feeling what a sneeze is to a cold. It's an outside manifestation of an inner conviction. Of course, all of this—the fear of appearing selfish and the deeper conviction that you are a failure—is *only one way to perceive yourself.* It is not the truth about you. You are not your fears. You also have the option of seeing the world another way, through your Wheel of Freedom.

The Wheel of Freedom

The Wheel of Freedom represents a choice that can lead to a new life. It is a set of decisions you can make that will help reinforce your higher self in order to change negative thoughts, feelings, and actions that are based on your fears. Most people assume that the Wheel of Freedom is the opposite of the Wheel of Fear. It is not. If the Wheel of Freedom were the opposite of the Wheel of Fear, the "selfish" person would combat her fears by replacing selfish behaviors with those she considered to be generous. But that's what she is already doing on the Wheel of Fear. Rather than the opposite of the Wheel of Fear, the Wheel of Freedom is an alternate to it.

The first step on the Wheel of Freedom is to identify your **essential nature.** I show you how to do this in *Fearless Living*. Your essential nature is the state of being that fuels your passion and gives you an abiding sense of purpose. It is, simply, the best part of yourself, the part that feels most complete and in tune. My clients have described their essential natures as authentic, creative, compassionate, accountable, courageous, and a long list of other traits. Naturally you can have more than one of these characteristics, yet there is one trait that helps to access all the rest. Once you pinpoint your essential nature, you can use it to put your Wheel of Freedom into motion.

The next step is to consciously engage in **proactive behavior** that stems from and supports your essential nature. For instance, if your essential nature is "compassion," you could consciously take actions that support your being kind to yourself and others. It could be a simple as taking a breath before making your next phone call. Resisting the urge to hurry up and take a shower when you really want a bath. Or it could also include reaching out to another. Perhaps asking a friend to do a dinner swap with you once a week. On Mondays, you make a double helping of dinner, one serving for your family and the other half for theirs, and on Wednesdays, your neighbor does the same for you. Maybe it is supporting a friend with an ill child even though the timing is inconvenient or seeing the rude bank teller as frustrated and very human. Instead of getting defensive, you smile at the teller anyway and decide not to let her mood affect your day.

Step three on the Wheel of Freedom happens once you have put your plans into action. For the first time, you have a sense of

wholeness. You are accessing your passion, creativity, inner joy and peace of mind. They are no longer haphazard feelings but daily experiences. You feel like your best self, and that gives you enormous power. It inspires you to take risks, it draws others to you, and it gives you the confidence and strength to move forward fearlessly.

Finally, the wholeness you experience from all these steps will steadily chip away at your fear of not being good enough. **Self-affirming behavior** will naturally, even unconsciously, spring from your conscious effort to be true to yourself. It is now easier to put yourself first without feeling selfish. And it is easier to be kind to others without being worried about being taken advantage of. Asking for help is no longer an effort or an embarrassment. And saying no doesn't include that twinge of guilt like it did before. And it is self-perpetuating—the more you take actions that align with your essential nature, the better you will feel, and the more often

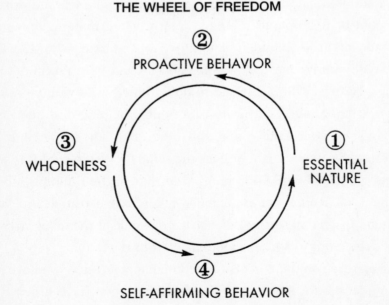

THE WHEEL OF FREEDOM

② PROACTIVE BEHAVIOR

③ WHOLENESS

① ESSENTIAL NATURE

④ SELF-AFFIRMING BEHAVIOR

you will be inspired to act with integrity, creativity, compassion, authenticity, or whatever you have singled out as your personal access point to the Wheel of Freedom.

With every encounter, every conversation, and every action, you have a choice. You can get caught on your Wheel of Fear or you can access your Wheel of Freedom. The interesting thing is, once you're aware of your Wheel of Fear, it becomes very hard to ignore. When you know what your fear trigger is, you can't help but recognize it. When you recognize it, you are instantly presented with a choice: fear or freedom? Choosing freedom can be difficult at first. If you have reacted out of fear all your life, you may not even know which words to use when you're coming from freedom—which is why I explain how to make the transition, step by step, in *Fearless Living*. You will know you're on the fearless path when you start experiencing states of mind that have eluded you before, such as satisfaction, focus, inner strength, detachment, acceptance, and a sense of abundance. Your life has truly become your own.

Gratitudes

Today, I am grateful for:

Brian Tart, vice president and editorial director of Dutton. A rare man fueled by passion and integrity who has kept every promise. I am grateful that we have once again joined forces on book number two. Your unwavering commitment inspires me.

Carole Baron, president of Dutton. Your kindness and support are blessings in my life. Thank you for opening your heart to Fearless Loving. I am grateful.

Elly Sidel, my agent and mentor, who has tirelessly dedicated herself to spreading the "Fearless" word. She has become more than an agent to me and I am extremely grateful for her honesty, tact, and love. My world would not be the same without you.

Lynette Padwa, my collaborator and now friend. A top-notch writer, editor, and brainstorming buddy who made book two effortless. Abundant thanks.

Amy Hughes, editorial assistant and now editor at Dutton. Her sunny disposition, spot-on comments and, overall support have made doing business a joy. A+!

Jennifer Repo, my past editor at Perigee Books. It was your insight and relentless commitment that put the Fearless series in motion. I will miss you.

Lisa Johnson, Kathleen Matthews, Erin Sinesky, Robert Kempe, Liz Perl, Beth Mellow, and the entire Fearless Loving PR team. It is an honor to work with a team that takes action, does what it says it is going to do and, bottom line, makes a difference. I am grateful you believe in my message and have taken it to heart. Thank you!

Aline Akelis, foreign rights agent at Dutton. Thank you for putting *Fearless Living* on the map in over twelve countries; I know *Fearless Loving* will spread through your efforts and care. And Melanie Koch, who relentlessly supported *Fearless Loving* in sub-rights. Thank you! Thank you!

Dutton sales staff. Double thanks go to the hard-working sales staff who have relentless taken care of *Fearless Living* and now *Fearless Loving*. It is appreciated.

Anna Cowles and the entire staff at Dutton, thank you! Thank you for your enthusiasm. Thank you for your commitment. Thank you for standing behind the vision of *Fearless Loving*.

Rowena Webb, Kerry Hood, Lisa Highton, and the rest of the staff at Hodder Headline in the United Kingdom and Australia, who have consistently put their hearts into *Fearless Loving*. Your care and support are gifts in my life. Thank you!

The entire staff at Talkback Productions and Channel 5 in the United Kingdom. We had an amazing time developing and producing *Life Doctor*. It is an experience I shall never forget. Special thanks go to Paul Franklin, my series producer; Kerry Scourfield, my right-hand gal who was in charge of keeping me sane during production; and Perry Harrison, a camera man who went above and beyond the call of duty. I appreciate your efforts in making sure I looked good, my friend! Double thanks go to Kim Peat, commissioning editor at Channel 5, and Daisy Goodwin, executive producer at Talkback Productions, who nurtured *Life Doctor* into reality. And to Sham Sandhu, Elin Parry, and the rest of the gang at Channel 5 and Talkback. Thank you!

Mark Austin Thomas, KLAC operations manager, who just knew I would make good radio. Robin Bertolucci, head honcho at KLAC, who said "yes." Thank you for holding the vision and supporting me as I learned the "art" of radio. Lastly, David Hall from Premiere Radio Network. Thank you for going out of your way for a beginner.

Wick Rowland, Jr.; Kim Johnson; Paula Roth; John Maginness; Shari Bernson; Dominic Dezzutti; and the entire staff at PBS, KBDI-TV in Denver. I am grateful for your support and your willingness to make magic together. Thank you for believing. I look forward to more. . . .

Greg Cortopassi, Kim Zoller, Nina Peterson, and the rest of the staff at Teamworks who devoted a year to breathing life into the Fearless Living Institute (FLI). Thank you.

Karen Thomas of Mile Hi, who stood by me and said, "Let me help." And you did. Thank you for your continuous cheerleading. It is appreciated. And special thanks go to Rev. Roger Teal for giving me an opportunity to *wow* his audience. I am blessed by your support. Lastly, my love goes to Rev. Michael Beckwith.

Jenna DeAngeles, graphic designer and friend. Your talent blows my mind and I look forward to the day, very soon, when the world will know you by name. It is an honor.

Sally Boccella, jack-of-all-trades. Your passionate support is a blessing. I am thankful for your enthusiasm, creative networking, and plain hard work. And to Brian, what a gem!

Faith Davis, for our weekly walks that keep me sane. Good to have you back in my life.

The Certified Fearless Living Coaches (CFLCs) who keep refining my coaching ability with their insights, tenaciousness and, consistent knocking to know more. You awaken more within me than I knew was possible. Thank you. And special thanks go to Cindee Ball, Stanley Otterstrom, and Bill Grout who have tirelessly volunteered their time to FLI. You never ask, "what," instead you ask "when." I am grateful.

The CFLCs who have dedicated their time to developing our coaches and helping FLI grow: Frank O'Hare, Janet Stilgoe, Robin Temple, Ruth Meinking, Lisa Barnett, and Jonna Lemes. I am blessed to know you.

The FLI core team: Marta Weiskopf, Michele Moore, Jerilyn Thiel, Trudy Arthurs, Susie Peterson, Lura Fischer, Mary Colwell, Cindy Tvinnereim, Rosemarie Lyall, and the rest of the FLI staff. Each of you has brought your unique talents to FLI and committed more of your heart that I ever dared dream. You inspire me daily.

Garrick Colwell, CEO and president of the Fearless Living Institute (FLI). Your dedication to FLI astonishes me, and your belief in me humbles me. Thank you for leaping into my world on faith.

Marta. Thank you for pushing me when I need a shove and pulling back when I need space. You are the mother I never had and I am grateful.

My dear sisters, Cindy and Linda, who had consistently supported me without hesitation. We have grown through much together and this I know without a doubt: I love you, No one can make me laugh like you do. No one can remind me of what matters most like you do. No one else can relax me with a phone call like you do. You are my anchor in my ever-expanding life. There is no way to thank you for all the gifts you have given me in this lifetime. So I simply say thank you! It is an honor to be called your sister.

No book is ever written alone. There are countless people who have supported me before, during, and after my first book, *Fearless Living,* and who have continued to be by my side during *Fearless Loving.* There are many people I thanked in *Fearless Living* and once again, I thank you. You know who you are.

We Want to hear From You. . . .

We'd love to know how *Fearless Loving* has changed your love life. Submit your Fearless Loving story at our Web site: www.FearlessLiving.org

Want *more* Fearless Loving?

Would you life to . . .

Attend a Fearless Loving workshop?
Consult a private Fearless Loving Coach?
Lead or join a Fearless Loving Fearbuster Group?
Call in to Rhonda's radio show?

For upcoming workshops, available private coaches, all the ins and outs of beginning your own Fearbuster Group, and, how to hear Rhonda on the radio, visit our Web site, www.FearlessLiving.org

Become A Fearless Living/Fearless Loving Coach

Help us spread the message of Fearless Loving! Become a Coach!

As the Fearless Living Institute has expanded into the United Kingdom, Australia, and beyond, we are committed to building a network of people dedicated to helping others decrease fear, whether in business or personal situations. Our extensive and in-depth coaching program will give you the skills and confidence to become a certified Fearless Living/Loving Coach, and work with individuals. And once you are a Coach, becoming a Trainer or Speaker is just an intention away. Visit www.FearlessLiving.org or call 303-447-2704

Bring the Fearless Message to Your Next Event. . . .

We are the gold standard for human development in the business world!

Fear-breaking topics range from Fearless Transitions to Fearless Leadership to Fearless Selling to Creating Accountability: The Fearless Approach to Empowering Your Employees, and more. The Fearless Living Institute has training that will fit any business that is interested in decreasing fear-based behaviors such as complaining, making excuses, blaming, etc., in the workplace. Benefits include: higher retention through increased employee and client satisfaction, increased staff productivity, and a renewed ability to tap into corporate creativity.

Keynotes, break-out sessions, trainings, and consulting available. Call the Fearless Living Institute at 303-447-2704

About the Author

Rhonda Britten, the foremost expert on fear, is the founder of the groundbreaking Fearless Living Institute, an organization dedicated to giving you the tools to master fear in business, at home, in your life. She is the author of *Fearless Living™: Live Without Excuses and Love Without Regret,* a pioneering work that has been translated into twelve languages, and *Fearless Loving: Eight Simple Truths That Will Change the Way You Date, Mate, and Relate,* a revolutionary path to love. On her weekly call-in radio show, broadcast from 570 KLAC in Los Angeles, she takes the mystery out of any challenge while showing her callers how to do it for themselves.

She has been featured on *Montel* and *Oprah,* profiled internationally in magazines such as *Shape, Marie Claire, You, She,* and *First for Women* and in newspapers such as the London *Sunday Times,* as well as on radio worldwide. On the small screen, Rhonda is the *Life Doctor,* a reality-based television show in the United Kingdom that transforms people's lives in thirty days.

Britten is an inspiring, informative, and empowering international speaker and Fearbuster Life and Career Coach who gives you practical tools to master the fear-based behaviors that stand in the way of your bottom-line success and personal fulfillment, showing you how to be on purpose, with purpose, fearlessly. Her repeat clients include Southwest Airlines, Dow Chemical, Blue Shield, Toyota, and Northrop Grumman, to name a few. Thousands have reaped the benefits of Rhonda's expertise, compassion, and insight.

For more information on Rhonda, contact the Fearless Living Institute at www.FearlessLiving.org, or call 303-447-2704

For additional Fearless support tools, products, and services visit www.FearlessLiving.org

Thank you for your support.
Stay Fearless!